handbook *for*
SPECIAL
NEEDS
coordinators

**The complete guide to your
role and responsibilities**

Jacquie Buttriss and Ann Callander

teacherbooks

© pfp publishing limited 2003

First published in Britain in 2003 by
pfp publishing limited
61 Gray's Inn Road
London WC1X 8TH

Editors and writers Jacquie Buttriss and Ann Callander
Contributors Robin Bartlett, Ann Berger, Sue Byron, Jane Calver,
Lynn Cousins, Diane Davies, Annabel Dixon, Sue Dow, Fiona Gibson,
Robin Hammerton, Beth Huke, Frances James, Julie Jennings,
Christine Khan, Jim Laing, Eithne Leming, Anne Phillips, Gillian Rees,
Graham Reeves, Christabel Reynish and Martin Skelton
Cover design PinkFrog
Page design Linda Reed and Associates

Printed and bound in the UK.

A catalogue record for this book is available from the British Library.

ISBN 1 874050 76 7

pfp orders and customer services
FREEPOST LON20579
London WC1X 8BR

Tel: 0845 602 4337   Fax: 0845 602 4338
www.pfp-publishing.com

Contents

Using this book

The *Handbook for Special Needs Coordinators* provides both an overview of the SEN scene and an in-depth guide to the day-to-day activities and responsibilities of an SEN coordinator. As well as being an informative read, it is intended for use as a dip-in resource by experienced and newly appointed SEN coordinators alike. Each chapter focuses on one major aspect of SEN and together they combine to provide a practical framework for addressing the needs of SEN children in primary school. This book is intended to be used together with its companion volume the *A–Z of Special Needs*, which is a definitive directory of SEN.

Everything in this book is built on the foundations laid by the 2001 SEN Code of Practice, implemented as from January 2002. The Code of Practice guides and underpins all the work the SEN coordinator is required to do in supporting SEN children. The extensive practical advice and strategies in this book address all the recommendations of the Code of Practice, as well as the more recent proposals (2002/3) to reform the way teachers and teaching assistants work in schools.

Chapters on the 2001 Code of Practice and inclusion are at the back of the book for ease of reference. If you are not already fully familiar with the Code and the principles of inclusion, it would be advisable to look at those chapters first, as they provide the context for everything else in the book.

This book has been written for SEN coordinators in primary schools. This will of course include those working in first, infant, junior and middle schools and there will also be an overlap with nurseries in Chapter 10: Early years and secondary schools in Chapter 11: Primary-secondary transition. If your school includes Reception children, and especially if it has a nursery attached, you will want to make use of the early years chapter. Similarly, if you are in a primary, junior or middle school, you will find it helpful to consider adopting some of the strategies suggested in the chapter on primary-secondary transition.

Both the authors have up-to-date school SEN coordinator and senior management experience and they bring to this book their 'chalk-face' understanding of just how challenging and demanding the role of the SEN coordinator can be and how much expertise it requires. However, they also know that, with the right support and practical advice, the SEN coordinator's role can often be the most rewarding job in the school.

We hope you will enjoy using this book. We don't expect you to read it through all at once – indeed, we're sure no SEN coordinator would be able to find the time to enjoy a concentrated read such as this! However, we are confident that it will become an invaluable guide to keep on your desk or bookshelf, ready to consult about any pressing SEN matter as it arises.

Finally, we would like to thank all those writers and professionals who have helped us to make this book as comprehensive and up-to-date as it is, especially those whose contributions we have credited at the end of each chapter. No SEN coordinator is an island! We are very grateful for their help.

Jacquie Buttriss and Ann Callander

CHAPTER 1

The role of the SEN coordinator

Whether you are an experienced SEN coordinator or someone new to the job, getting to grips with what your role actually is will be an ongoing issue.

Over the past few years, the role of SEN coordinator has taken on a new significance. The responsibilities involved are both extensive and complex, with the requirement to have both knowledge and understanding of a wide range of special needs problems and conditions, as well as the practical resources to cater for all – or at least to know where to go for help.

> 'The SEN Coordinator, in collaboration with the headteacher and governing body, plays a key role in determining the strategic development of the SEN policy and provision in the school in order to raise the achievement of children with SEN.' (DfES, 2001 – 5:30)

The National Standards

The best place to get an overview of the role of the SEN coordinator is the *National Standards for Special Educational Needs Coordinators* published by the TTA. While they don't explain in detail what your day to day tasks and responsibilities are, they do set out the professional knowledge, understanding, skills and attributes needed to carry out the role of SEN coordinator and state that 'It is the sum of these aspects which defines the expertise demanded of the role.' (TTA, 1998 – foreword)

Professional knowledge and understanding
You should have up-to-date knowledge of developments in education generally and special education in particular. It is also expected that your knowledge and understanding can be applied within the different aspects of the role.

Skills and attributes
A SEN coordinator should have

- leadership skills
- professional competence
- decision-making skills (the ability to solve problems and make decisions)

- communication skills (the ability to make points clearly and to listen to and understand the views of others)
- self-management skills (the ability to plan time effectively and to organise oneself well)
- a range of personal attributes displayed by all successful and effective teachers.

Key areas of SEN coordination
These set out the key responsibilities of the SEN coordinator under the headings

- Strategic direction and development of SEN provision
- Teaching and learning
- Leading and managing staff
- Efficient and effective deployment of staff and resources.

This might seem daunting but the National Standards also assume a high level of support for the SEN coordinator from the headteacher, governors and senior management and this is reflected in the key outcomes of SEN coordination.

You'll find the National Standards useful as they provide a structured approach to performance management and they support both you and the headteacher in setting targets, evaluating progress and identifying future development.

The 2001 Code of Practice builds on the National Standards in providing a fuller framework for your role. It also makes it clear that one of the main features of the role is to work alongside colleagues to develop effective ways of teaching in order to help children overcome barriers to learning. You are given a proactive management role in order to ensure that all children receive sustained effective teaching and make good progress towards their targets.

Key responsibilities

SEN coordinators should, of course, ensure that they have a good knowledge and understanding of special educational needs, but it is also important that they develop expertise in leadership and management. You have a key role to play in motivating and guiding colleagues and in disseminating examples of effective teaching, not only for children with special needs but for all children. The 2001 Code of Practice identifies the key responsibilities for SEN coordinators.

> ### Key responsibilities
>
> 'In mainstream primary schools the key responsibilities of the SEN coordinator may include
> - overseeing the day to day operation of the school's SEN policy
> - co-ordinating provision for children with special educational needs
> - liaising with and advising fellow teachers
> - managing learning support assistants
> - overseeing the records of all children with special educational needs
> - liaising with parents of children with special educational needs
> - contributing to the in-service training of staff
> - liaising with external agencies including the LEA's support and educational psychology services, health and social services, and voluntary bodies.'
>
> (DfES, 2001 – 5:32)

Professional development

Being able to consistently meet your key responsibilities means keeping up to date and that means your own professional development is very important. But what should you focus on and how can you make sure your development is effective and current?

Development can take many forms and will be influenced by both personal and school-based factors, as well as by local and national initiatives.

Whatever form of professional development you choose to undertake, and for whatever reason, the crucial thing, if it is to be a positive and useful experience, is that you should want to do it and that you should want to make good use of it.

> 'Good professionals are engaged in a journey of self-improvement, always ready to reflect on their own practice in the light of other approaches and to contribute to the development of others by sharing their best practice and insights. They learn from what works.' (DfEE, 2000)

The first step in planning your own professional development will be to review your own and your school's needs. There are three main aspects of this review.

1 Your development

The first aspect is to focus on your own strengths and interests and what you might need to do to ensure that you keep fully up to date with these aspects of your role. Self-review will be a fundamental element of your appraisal, as part of the performance management process. Additionally, self-review may follow on from an inspection by Ofsted or whole-school self-evaluation, or it may simply come out of your own personal self-review. Use the following checklist to help.

- Have there been any recent research findings or initiatives to keep abreast of in any of your main areas of expertise?
- Have there been any new books or articles published in these areas?
- Are there any newly available teaching or learning materials to investigate?
- Are there any recognised experts in any of these fields who are due to be speaking within easy travelling distance?
- Are you confident in delivering training to colleagues within your school? Are there any presentation skills which you would like to learn and which might help you with training and also with presentations to parents?
- Do your ICT skills enable you to make full use of all the appropriate support materials available to SEN coordinators on the Internet? Are you able to use software to support children with their learning needs, to make use of computers for assessment purposes and to use appropriate data handling, target setting, reporting and IEP writing packages?

2 Children's needs

The next area for consideration is the range of children's needs, for which you may be asked to offer help and advice within your school.

- Do you have children in your school with any specific problems, about which you might wish to find out more?
- Are there any ongoing concerns about how your school approaches certain aspects of special needs work (for example, the organisation of learning support)?

- Are there any whole-school issues (such as behaviour management) which you could take as a key issue for your own professional development?

- Would it be helpful to see how other schools and units tackle certain difficulties?

- Would a visit to a resource centre be useful in locating appropriate support materials for your children?

- Do any of your physically disabled children need adaptations to their environment which are currently in use elsewhere?

- Are you able to liaise with SEN coordinators in other local schools on a regular basis?

- Are there any local outreach facilities which you would like to know more about?

3 School needs

Last, but equally crucial in the review process, you will want to give consideration to the needs of colleagues, both teaching and non-teaching.

- Are you able to support and advise colleagues as effectively as you would wish?

- How do other schools organise their teaching assistants (TAs) most effectively?

- Would training needs be better met by going to courses of a general nature elsewhere, or would it be more appropriate to deliver some relevant in-school training for teaching assistants or for the teaching staff as a whole?

Types of professional development

An important part of your role is to be aware of the range of professional development that is available, in order to be able to meet the needs of the children and staff in the school.

Courses

Types of courses include the following.

- Courses delivered by your local LEA, other training providers or professional organisations. These can be on both specific and general SEN topics.

- Accredited courses, working towards a specific award or qualification. (You will be expected to produce written evidence of both practical and theoretical research.)

- Courses run by professionals (eg. speech and language therapists). These courses provide very specific support and advice in specialist areas.

Membership of professional bodies

Professional bodies, such as the National Association for Special Educational Needs (NASEN), the Dyslexia Society and other support agencies, all issue informative publications and newsletters giving details of current SEN issues, research briefs and courses available.

INSET

Shared federation, pyramid or cluster INSET, or other local INSET and liaison forums allow small schools to take part in affordable SEN INSET. They provide a focus for the staff of feeder schools and upper schools to work together, and they also provide opportunities for the sharing of expertise. Such informal groupings can also be an invaluable opportunity for SEN coordinators to discuss experiences and situations, compare notes and share approaches.

Conferences

There are various national conferences with a specific SEN focus.

Resource centres and exhibitions

Visits to resource centres or exhibitions will offer valuable opportunities to keep up to date on the latest resources.

Visits and observation

Visits to schools or units that are centres of good practice give you the opportunity to look for innovative ideas and ways of working that will relate to your own school's needs. Observation or modelling of good SEN practice within the school will often work best if it is seen as a sharing of ideas. You can also carry out classroom-based research, which may be linked to an accredited course.

Reading

Read journals and publications relating to SEN issues (and possibly set up an SEN library in your school).

Internet

Access SEN websites for research into specific conditions. An excellent website for links to a huge range of SEN organisations, support materials, information for SEN coordinators and more is the DfES site (www.dfes.gov.uk/sen/senhome). This site has links to organisations such as NASEN and the SEN Coordinator Forum, an information exchange for SEN coordinators. Another excellent website listing SEN organisations is www.becta.org.uk/inclusion.

SEN networks

The pressures of the SEN coordinator's role can often be difficult to explain to teaching colleagues in your school, so it is extremely important that you build and develop support networks with other SEN coordinators and SEN professionals in your area to share the joys and the difficulties that you encounter in your role

In some local authorities there are regular, termly meetings for all SEN coordinators, run by an advisor or LEA staff member. A typical agenda includes the passing on of LEA information, followed by a shared session. This could be something topical, such as an opportunity to review new legislation, or an aspect of SEN agreed by the group at its previous meeting.

NASEN is probably the best-known support group. It offers information and advice to teachers, parents and anyone else interested in a wide range of needs. The association funds research, publishes books and sponsors events. It also publishes several journals, including the British Journal of Special Education, Support for Learning, the British Journal of Learning Support and the Journal of Research in Special Educational Needs. Its website www.nasen.org.uk provides links to other sites of interest to those involved with special needs.

The Special Educational Needs Joint Initiative for Training (SENJIT) offers courses and support groups for teachers and local authorities, particularly in the light of new legislation or government requirements for schools. SENJIT is based at the Institute of Education in London and has a website at www.ioe.ac.uk/teepnnp/SENJIT–Home.html.

Time management

The 2001 Code of Practice acknowledges that the role of the SEN coordinator 'is time consuming and therefore it is usually inappropriate for the SEN coordinator to have other school-wide responsibilities.' (DfES, 2001 – 5:34)

In a large school it is feasible to create regular, timetabled sessions for an SEN coordinator to carry out all of his or her responsibilities. However, it is not always possible for heads and governors to allocate sufficient time in smaller schools. The most effective way of allocating time, when the SEN coordinator is a class teacher in a small school, is for the headteacher to share some of the responsibilities.

Teamwork

Any SEN coordinator needs to be part of a good team, however small, in order to make effective use of the time available. The team will consist of all those people who have contact with children with special needs. Everyone will have some part to play in making sure that effective provision is organised for the children who have been identified at School Action and School Action Plus.

The **headteacher** can

- contact outside agencies (they are often not available during breaktimes or lunchtimes)
- organise and chair multi-professional meetings (the headteacher usually needs to be present in any case)
- monitor the progress of children identified as having special needs, as part of a whole-school monitoring process.

The **class teacher** can

- keep a notebook to jot down any achievements or difficulties encountered, in order to inform the review of a child's individual education plan (IEP)
- photocopy a few examples of children's work as evidence of their achievements and to inform next step targets
- gather appropriate information from parents.

The **teaching assistant** can

- deliver specific programmes of support – these may involve speech and language, occupational therapy, literacy, numeracy, etc. (some may require training from outside agencies)
- talk to the children about their IEP targets (helping them to identify next-step targets)
- organise and catalogue learning resources
- undertake administrative tasks – consortium orders, photocopying, mounting display work.

Parents or carers can

- support their child with one target on the IEP (you or the class teacher will need to make sure that the target is clearly understood)
- keep a notebook to jot down any achievements or difficulties encountered, in order to inform the review of an IEP (although not all parents will want to be involved to this extent)
- share their child's home achievements which may be in a field of activity of which the school is not aware.

Streamlining your work

To help make best use of the time available to you, consider these ways of grouping together work and meetings in order to avoid repetition.

- Try to hold group meetings with several staff members when you want to talk about children with similar learning difficulties.

- Identify common staff INSET needs and ask for time to be allocated during staff meetings for you to deliver school-based SEN INSET or to invite outside professionals to talk to staff.

- Review IEPs with both parents and class teachers at the termly parents' evening, if possible. (This will depend on your not being a class teacher yourself.) It may be advisable to allow for longer appointment times.

- Try to integrate the annual review with existing review systems within your school, in order to avoid duplication of requests for information and attendance at meetings.

- Try to hold group annual reviews on the same day for some statemented children, if you have a number in the school. Negotiate with key professionals to attend on that day. In this way you can avoid having to negotiate individual times with a variety of agencies.

- Try to give one SEN teaching assistant the specific responsibility of coordinating support materials so that all staff know who to contact.

Simple time-management tips

- Keep a small diary to hand to write down meeting times, visits from outside professionals and other important dates (you may be teaching when the message arrives and it can be easy to double-book).

- Carry a tape recorder, particularly at break times when colleagues make requests, and make quick oral notes on questions and queries.

- Give each class teacher a list of children in the class who need to be supported through School Action or School Action Plus, highlighting their strengths and learning difficulties.

- Give each class teacher a folder with brief descriptions of some of the key learning difficulties they may encounter, plus some suggested teaching strategies (see the Chapter 4: Strategies for learning).

- When talking to parents, always identify children's achievements before you identify their difficulties. It is easy to waste good parental liaison time if parents feel anxious and worried.

SEN policy

The school governors have a responsibility to develop and monitor the school's SEN policy, in consultation with the headteacher and the SEN coordinator. You will have a key role to play in evaluating and reviewing the policy.

The Code of Practice states that 'The SEN policy **must** contain the information as set out in the Education (Special Educational Needs) (Information) (England) Regulations 1999 at Annex A.' (DfES, 2001 – 1:24)   *Annex A*

The main areas detailed in this document are

- basic information about the school's special education provision

- information about the school's policies for the identification and assessment of and provision for all children with special educational needs

- information about the school's staffing policies and partnership with bodies beyond the school.

It is not essential that your policy arranges information in the same order as is described in Annex A, but the advantage of doing so is that it makes it easier for you to check that everything is covered.

SEN policy pointers

A good SEN policy

- reflects the practice and aspirations of the whole school

- is accessible to all members of the school community

- helps to secure the necessary provision for children with SEN

- embodies the arrangements for evaluating the success of the policy

- clearly sets out its purpose

- identifies the criteria used to determine how funding is allocated

- describes the criteria used to identify children who are identified as having special needs

- gives teachers clear guidance about how SEN is coordinated and managed within the school and what is expected of class teachers

- reflects the LEA policy

- gives parents clear guidance on how the school will act on parental concerns and provide support to their child where necessary.

SEN provision

When you review and update your school's SEN policy you will be evaluating how it supports SEN provision within your school. The special educational needs of the vast majority of children will be met within a mainstream setting. It is only for a small minority of children that LEAs are called upon to determine and arrange specialist SEN provision. The Code of Practice recommends that there be a graduated response to children's needs and that they should only be identified as having special needs if the nature of intervention is 'additional to or different from those provided as part of the school's usual differentiated curriculum.' (DfES, 2001 – 5:43)

It is the responsibility of the SEN coordinator to ensure that provision for an SEN child matches the nature of their needs. The decision to make SEN provision available for a child has important implications for the child, the parents, the teachers and sometimes the LEA.

Inclusive provision

It is not enough that children are present in mainstream classrooms and receiving additional SEN provision. It is important that the provision is inclusive rather than exclusive and relates to the child's learning with the class as well as to his or her individual needs.

> ### Principles of SEN provision
> SEN provision must build upon the principles stated in the National Curriculum on how to plan a more inclusive curriculum. These are
> - setting suitable learning targets
> - responding to children's diverse learning needs
> - overcoming potential barriers to learning.

Monitoring provision

Class teachers benefit from the fact that the detailed assessment and tracking of children with SEN is overseen and monitored by a colleague with more experience and knowledge of what action needs to be taken.

As SEN coordinator you need to

- gather information from the class teacher about the child's previous educational experience
- observe the child's approach to learning within the classroom setting
- highlight general areas of difficulty for early intervention

- identify the child's areas of strength
- suggest general intervention techniques and set targets
- involve the child in target setting when possible
- use diagnostic tests to identify specific areas of difficulty
- suggest specific intervention techniques and set targets
- use evidence such as baseline, curricular and standardised tests to monitor progress
- have regular discussions with the class teacher, teaching assistant and parents on the outcomes of interventions
- involve parents in developing a partnership approach to the child's learning.

Adequate progress

Ensuring that effective provision is made for children with special educational needs is a complex and time-intensive task, requiring regular and consistent monitoring and review. Provision can only be judged to be effective if the children are making adequate progress. The Code of Practice defines 'adequate progress' in a number of ways. Adequate progress might be

'progress which
- closes the attainment gap between the child and their peers
- prevents the attainment gap growing wider
- is similar to that of peers starting from the same attainment baseline, but less than that of the majority of peers
- matches or betters the child's previous rate of progress
- ensures access to the full curriculum
- demonstrates an improvement in self-help, social or personal skills
- demonstrates improvements in the child's behaviour.'
(DfES, 2001 – 5:42)

The SEN budget

In order to coordinate special needs provision effectively, you need to be aware of the sources of SEN funding, the formula used in your area and the amount allocated to your school. Although it may not be your direct role to manage the SEN budget, you nevertheless have an important part to play in advising the senior management team and the finance committee with regard to SEN spending.

You may need to advise on

- staffing needs (particularly the number of teaching assistants required)
- staff training and INSET
- school-based SEN initiatives (setting up an SEN library, providing a time-out room)
- ICT resources for SEN support
- curriculum and administrative resources
- resources to support physical and sensory needs (ramps, special chairs, sensory equipment).

SEN has a different funding basis from most other areas within school, and there are a number of different ways that money may come into a school budget.

1 **Delegated budget** Direct funding from the local education authority.

2 **The Standards Fund** A collection of specific grants aimed at educational improvements in areas such as literacy, numeracy and social inclusion. Both schools and LEAs can bid for government money from the Standards Fund.

3 **National Lottery** SEN funding comes particularly from the New Opportunities Fund and the National Endowment for Science, Technology and the Arts.

4 **European funding**

5 **Trust funds** These will often give small-scale awards to local schools for books, equipment and resources.

The main source of funding for maintained schools is through a direct funding mechanism from the LEA. This is on the basis of the number of children on roll, with special educational needs taken into account.

All local authorities have their own formula for delegating money to schools, and SEN always has a specific allocation. Although based partly on the number of children on roll, LEAs also use a number of other factors to assess need. The one most commonly used is the number of children who are entitled to free school meals. This may seem a random link but research over a number of years has consistently shown that this indicator is correlated with the level of special educational need. Schools with a high percentage of children entitled to free school meals (over 30 per cent) are likely to have a high level of special needs. Other factors used by LEAs include end of key stage test results, low verbal reasoning scores, public examination results and percentage of children with English as an additional language.

Some LEAs keep a fund to support inclusion of children with high-level difficulties. Money has to be applied for on an individual basis and is often the subject of an LEA audit.

Within even the wealthiest schools, money and resources are always limited. Schools have to prioritise, depending on their needs. Therefore it's important to set out needs and priorities in the school improvement plan so that they are clear to everyone.

SEN action plan

As SEN coordinator you should be aware of the amount of money allocated to the SEN budget, even if you are not directly responsible for the way in which this allocation is made. At the beginning of the year you need to draw up an action plan. It's helpful to think of things in terms of short, medium and long-term priorities and how much each will cost. Decide which actions or resources are essential, or have been carried over from the previous year. These are your short-term priorities.

Medium-term plans may be resources or initiatives that are set to begin later in the year. They could also include extending specific resources that are already in place. It may be that you are not able to achieve all your medium-term plans in one financial year.

Long-term plans are a good way of setting out a 'wish list' of things you would like to do if the money were to become available. It's helpful for the senior management team and the governing body to be aware of what you are planning or would like to do. It allows you to set out your vision of special needs provision within the school and enables them to make more informed choices when allocating budgets. You also need to reserve some money for contingencies that may arise during the year. If it is not needed for unforeseen expenditure towards the end of the financial year, you are then free to spend it on your long-term plans.

Your action plan should be discussed and agreed with the head and the senior management team and be reviewed by the SEN governor.

Budgeting time

A budget involves areas other than the simply financial. Time is probably the most expensive teacher commodity, and that which is in shortest supply. Include a time element with your budget, including costing in your own time. If you are planning to implement a new programme of IEP reviews, for example, you may want to buy in supply cover to release class teachers, teaching assistants and yourself.

Monitoring value for money

In order to monitor the effectiveness of SEN resourcing you will need to keep your own records. Your school administration officer is probably the person who keeps track of orders and invoices for materials ordered on a day-to-day basis, but you will need to keep a note of all SEN spending, detailing dates and costs.

If you have been working to an action plan drawn up at the beginning of the year, the task of monitoring towards the end of the financial year is a fairly straightforward one. You need to check whether you were able to meet the priorities that you set and whether there were any unforeseen contingencies that took money from the budget.

If you have bought specific resources for the school, it's worth making a brief evaluation of them, after consultation with colleagues, to show how useful they have been and what they have achieved. It is important that you involve colleagues when evaluating teaching resources in order to ensure that the materials are being used effectively – to support children's progress. This measure is known as value for money.

Liaising with and advising fellow teachers

An important part of your role as SEN coordinator is providing advice and support to your colleagues so that they can work to meet the special educational needs of the children they teach. Many teachers struggle alone with children they are concerned about, often believing that the fault lies in their teaching. They may need guidance on

- how to identify children with special educational needs
- how to plan to meet those needs
- organisational and teaching strategies
- how to involve parents
- how to communicate information
- how to work with other professionals and agencies
- how to monitor and record progress.

As SEN coordinator, you are the first port of call for a class teacher who is concerned about a child in their class. It is vital that teachers can talk to you informally about children's needs – perhaps over a cup of coffee in the staffroom – to discuss initial concerns and decide together what action to take. You need to find out

- why the class teacher is concerned about this particular child
- how long the class teacher has been concerned
- whether other teachers have expressed similar concerns
- whether, in the class teacher's opinion, the difficulties the child is experiencing are over and above those that are likely to be met by simple differentiation in the classroom
- whether the child's performance is significantly below that of other children in the class.

You may have to help colleagues to understand that not every discussion about a child will lead to the child being identified as having special educational needs. You need to assure them that they can air concerns informally at any time and that the experience and advice of other colleagues will also be of benefit.

Identification and assessment of special needs

If it is established through discussion that a child is experiencing learning difficulties, you will then need to start the identification and assessment process. Now is the time to gather as much information as possible to help pinpoint specific needs and identify the support required. It's good practice for the class teacher to meet the child's parents to discuss the initial concerns and explain the next steps that could be taken. There is no need for you to be present but it's an immense support to the class teacher if you advise them on how to approach the discussion and deal with any queries.

With the help of the class teacher you will need to gather relevant information that may help to identify specific needs. These may be

- school records such as reports
- medical records, in order to rule out a physical problem (it might be worth organising sight and hearing tests if this hasn't already been done)
- reports from any other agencies
- results of end of key stage assessments (if available or applicable)
- other test results (if available or applicable)
- attendance records
- parents' opinions, such as on behaviour at home or attitudes to school

- notes of observations of the child made at school – these will demonstrate typical behaviour and could shed light on any difficulties.

There also need to be regular and formal meetings between class teachers and the SEN coordinator so that information can be shared and difficulties evaluated on a regular basis.

SEN library and staff training

Your colleagues look to you as SEN coordinator to keep them up-to-date and informed about SEN issues. Your role involves being able to offer a certain amount of SEN training. You will not be expected to be an expert in all areas but you will be expected to put staff in contact with external specialists. Sometimes this could be suggesting that staff read a particular book or leaflet in the SEN library. You can start a lending library quite inexpensively by sending for information leaflets and buying booklets from support agencies (for addresses see the *A–Z of Special Needs*, also from pfp publishing). Leaflets should relate to the different special needs in your school and be available to parents if appropriate.

To further your colleagues' understanding of SEN issues or conditions, you may be asked to

- contribute to SEN training at staff meetings
- lead twilight sessions
- organise training sessions to be delivered by external agencies
- contribute to INSET days
- organise SEN INSET days.

Identifying targets and preparing an individual education plan (IEP)

This is the area in which you can be of most use to your colleagues. If possible, you should work with a colleague to identify targets and write the plan. In larger schools with many members of staff this may not always be practical on a one-to-one basis but it is still useful to work in small groups, especially when several teachers are dealing with similar difficulties. Some schools have designated staff meeting time for teachers to write and update IEPs, with the SEN coordinator available to assist them.

It's important to try to review an IEP and compose the next one in the same sitting, so that you can discuss what has worked and what hasn't and bear that in mind for the future. Target-setting causes many non-specialist teachers the most difficulty in

preparing an IEP. If teachers learn to see target-setting as part of the everyday assessment process and not as something peculiar to special needs, then they should find it less of a problem. Setting learning targets for an IEP is no different from making an assessment of a child's progress, identifying their next steps and then planning work accordingly.

An IEP is a key document for a child with special educational needs. But it is only really useful if it is used as a working document by all the adults involved with the child's progress and if the learning targets are monitored carefully. The real measure of the success of an IEP is the individual progress of the child against his or her own individual targets, rather than against external criteria.

Key points for IEPs

A good IEP has a number of features, including

- [ ] identifying the exact nature and extent of the child's learning difficulty
- [ ] specifying the criteria against which success can be measured, which can be easily understood by all those involved, including the child if appropriate
- [ ] saying what additional resources should be used
- [ ] indicating how parents are to be involved
- [ ] tying in with the normal classroom routines and procedures within the school
- [ ] specifying only that which is 'additional to or different from' the normal differentiated provision for all children.

For a sample format for an IEP, see Chapter 2: Plan, do, review.

IEPs in the 2001 Code of Practice

The Code of Practice states that an IEP 'should include information about

- [ ] the short-term targets set for or by the child
- [ ] the teaching strategies to be used
- [ ] the provision to be put in place
- [ ] when the plan is to be reviewed
- [ ] success and/or exit criteria
- [ ] outcomes (to be recorded when IEP is reviewed).'(DfES, 2001 – 5:50)

The Code also notes that IEPs

'should be crisply written and focus on three or four individual targets, chosen from those relating to the key areas of communication, literacy, numeracy, behaviour and social skills that match the child's needs.'(DfES, 2001 – 5:51).

The SEN coordinator has a key role in monitoring the IEP, but all those involved with the child should contribute to it, and the child should be helped to understand how the IEP is being used to help them make progress. teaching assistants often have valuable insights which can make significant contributions to the recognition of a child's progress.

Monitoring IEP progress

Useful approaches to monitoring the progress towards the targets on an IEP include

- the completion of a checklist by a TA on a daily basis
- a discussion on a weekly basis between the class teacher, the child and the TA, with some brief notes to act as a record for parents
- guided group teaching by the SEN coordinator or class teacher
- sample monitoring by the SEN coordinator through informal observation.

As a result of differing approaches to IEP monitoring, targets are reviewed at varying intervals. For some targets, particularly behavioural targets, weekly or even daily monitoring might be called for. If the targets are learning targets, then termly monitoring is more reasonable. For an individual child it might be appropriate to have constant, positive feedback on what is being achieved, especially where precision teaching is used.

Even when targets have been specifically identified and individual education plans have been carefully written to describe the strategies to meet the targets, your colleagues will continue to need your support on the day-to-day management of children with special educational needs in the classroom and this includes the organising of teaching assistants.

Managing teaching assistants

The appointment of teaching assistants is generally undertaken by the headteacher and the SEN governor, though you may well be asked to be on the panel selecting or interviewing teaching assistants. You will probably be their line manager, so it makes sense for you to be involved in their appointment.

The management of teaching assistants is an important part of your role as SEN coordinator. In appointing and deploying teaching assistants, you will need to balance the needs of all SEN children. In most cases teaching assistants will not be available to work with classes full time. If you only have a few teaching assistants to share between several classes

you will need to prioritise where they work. You need to deploy your teaching assistants where you feel they will most benefit the children and don't just allocate their time to classes equally. If there is more need in one class than another, give those children more time. Some teaching assistants will be employed to support an individual child and it is the responsibility of the SEN coordinator to advise on appropriate support strategies for that child, both to the class teacher and to the teaching assistant.

⚠ LSAs

In this book we use the term teaching assistant (TA), but the term learning support assistant (LSA) is also widely used for a TA who specialises in supporting SEN children, either individually or in groups. These job titles are defined in more depth in Chapter 5: Teaching assistants.

Managing SEN records

The way in which records are kept varies from school to school and is often affected by the guidance or requirements of the LEA. Keeping everything up-to-date can be a time-consuming activity. Yet it is an important activity, which enables you and your colleagues to monitor progress and evaluate the effectiveness of what you do to meet children's general and specific needs.

The efficient maintenance of SEN records also helps you to provide accurate information and evidence to parents, professionals and other agencies.

'... schools should record the steps taken to meet the needs of individual children. The school's SEN coordinator should have responsibility for ensuring that the records are properly kept and available as needed ... The information collected should reveal the different perceptions of those concerned with the child, any immediate educational concerns and an overall picture of the child's strengths and weaknesses.' (DfES, 2001 – 5:24–26)

Keeping good records

SEN children's records should include

- ☐ the child's IEPs
- ☐ assessment data
- ☐ reports from external agencies
- ☐ school reports
- ☐ record of achievement (showing evidence of strengths)
- ☐ portfolio of work (showing progress over time).

SEN liaison

Partnership between parents, children, schools, LEAs and other agencies is one of the principles of the Code of Practice.

Liaison with parents

You certainly won't be personally and directly involved in all contacts with parents. However, you do need to make sure that there are proper procedures in place so that parents are

- aware of what to do if they think their child might have special educational needs
- agreeable to and involved in the assessment of their child's needs
- able to contribute to IEP targets
- kept informed about the action the school will be taking through their child's IEP
- provided with advice about how they can help their child at home
- able to contribute to termly reviews
- aware of where and how they can obtain further information and advice.

As SEN coordinator you will need to develop good relationships with parents at an early stage. Informal, friendly approaches are important as this helps to allay parental anxieties and gives them confidence to take an active part in supporting their child at home. Liaison with parents is an important aspect of your role. See also Chapter 7: Working with parents.

Liaison with governors

The Code states that 'All maintained school governing bodies have important statutory duties towards pupils with special educational needs.' (DfES, 2001 – 1:16) SEN coordinators are accountable to the governing body and have a duty to keep them informed of SEN initiatives in the school.

Most schools appoint a governor with responsibility for special needs. As SEN coordinator it is important that you meet with the SEN governor on a regular basis in order to discuss issues regarding provision. In this way you can ensure that the SEN governor is able to make relevant decisions when working with the headteacher on the SEN budget. Liaison with governors is another essential aspect of the SEN coordinator's role. See also Chapter 9: Working with governors.

Liaison with external agencies

Liaising with external agencies can be a time-consuming aspect of your role, but it is an essential part. It is extremely useful to have a list of the relevant external agencies, detailing their names, addresses, telephone numbers and their roles.

There are very good practical reasons why you should maintain good links with external agencies. You might need

- advice and support in the assessment of children's needs
- assistance in meeting children's needs
- specialist information about procedures
- in-service training for yourself and/or your colleagues
- to advise parents on who to contact for further information and assistance.

How you liaise with the external agencies will vary according to their own procedures, and perhaps also according to the requirements of your LEA. However, it is useful to make contact and establish good relationships with the various individuals even when you have no immediate need of their services. Then, when the need does arise, you will be able to act quickly.

It's also worth having established procedures within your school about who actually makes contact and how such contact is established and recorded. That way, you can avoid mixed messages and the sort of confusion that can be caused when clear procedures don't exist.

Multi-professional consultation meetings are organised in a number of LEAs. They are usually held twice a year and attended by a number of external specialists, plus the headteacher of the school and the SEN coordinator. These meetings allow schools to raise whole-school SEN issues, discuss the progress of individual children and identify staff training needs. You are expected to prepare the agenda for these meetings and report back to the SEN governor and the senior management team.

The relevant professionals can be alerted and consulted at these meetings if you are considering asking for a formal assessment of a child's special educational needs from the LEA.

Preparing for a statement of special educational need

When it becomes clear that a child's needs are so great that they cannot be met without specific provision beyond School Action Plus, these needs are set out in a statement. A statement establishes the child's rights to this provision, safeguarding them by setting out what the needs are and how they should be provided for. It is a shared document that is drawn up after consultation with all those involved with the child.

A statement of special educational need is a legal document. It involves a good deal of administrative work on the part of the school and the LEA, and it is not issued lightly or easily. There are usually financial implications for both the school and the LEA once a statement has been issued.

A request for a statutory assessment can be made by a school, by a parent or by another agency. However, the most common route is at a review that includes all of the agencies supporting or advising the child, as well as the parents. If this recommendation is made at a meeting of professionals without the parents, then they must be consulted before any further action is taken. These steps should be followed.

Step 1

The SEN coordinator, or whoever has been liaising with the parents, needs to arrange a meeting to go through the concerns, clarifying the procedures and timetables that are involved in applying for a statement. Many parents are pleased that a statement will ensure continued support for their child. However, for others, a statement may be seen as a label, or a diagnosis that they may not yet have accepted. There may be a period of denial or, at best, of needing to come to terms with the fact that their child is in some way different from others. You must handle this with sensitivity.

Step 2

The school should refer to LEA guidelines to ensure that the child meets the criteria to move beyond School Action Plus. Many LEAs have clear procedures for moving on to statutory assessment. The specifics will differ from one authority to another, but much of the necessary process will be the same. Although there may already be a lot of documentation about the child, this is the point at which an assessment is made of the information from everyone who has been involved with them.

Step 3

Once there is agreement from the parents, the school makes a formal request to the LEA for the child's needs to be considered for a statement. The school has to give as much information as possible about the history of the child's needs. This request will also provide evidence that the school has made consistent attempts to meet the child's needs from within its own resources. A statement not only ensures provision for an individual child, it also guarantees a level of funding for the school. However, this depends on the way that each LEA has delegated SEN funding. If a high level of funding has been delegated to schools, then the school may be expected to fund any provision named on the statement. Schools need to work closely with LEAs over the matter of making reasonable provision within given budgets. The Code of Practice gives advice on the matter of funding provision in paragraphs 8:12 to 8:14.

In some circumstances the parents may be unwilling for the school to proceed with a formal request. If this is the case, the school should set out the reasons for requesting a statement, making clear the parents' reservations, and leave it to the LEA to take over the liaison with parents.

Step 4

Once a request for statutory assessment has been made, the LEA has to respond within six weeks, giving an answer to the request as well as the reasons for the decision that has been made.

The statutory assessment process

Once a decision has been made to go ahead with the statutory assessment process, the LEA has a duty to seek written information about the child from

- parents
- the school or education provider
- the health authority (usually the child's GP or consultant)
- a psychologist (usually the school's educational psychologist)
- social services
- any other agencies involved with the child.

When the people listed above are asked for their advice on a child, further time constraints apply. The LEA has ten weeks in which to request advice, consider that advice and make its assessment, so agencies will be given a deadline for their response. The whole process, from the initial request to the final outcome, should take no more than 26 weeks.

A prompt sheet to help you provide information about a child is provided on pages 25–26.

The final outcome will either be the issuing of a statement, or a notice to parents giving reasons for not issuing a statement.

The statutory assessment time line

The LEA receives and responds to a request for statutory assessment.	**six weeks**
The LEA seeks and considers advice from all agencies and informs them of the decision as to whether or not it will proceed with an assessment.	**ten weeks**
The LEA draws up a proposed statement.	**two weeks**
Parents and other agencies consider the proposed statement before it is issued as a final statement.	**eight weeks**

Once a child's needs have been agreed, it is necessary to decide how to meet those needs.

Provision made by the school

The child may be with you for some years, so don't commit yourself and the school to things that you won't be able to continue. However, don't forget the obvious things that you do as a matter of course, such as

- regular liaison with parents and other agencies
- participation in multi-agency planning and review meetings
- providing opportunities for the child to develop self-esteem.
- providing opportunities for the child to produce work in a variety of different ways.

Provision made by external agencies

This is your opportunity to set out what additional provision you think would be helpful, such as a teaching assistant. However, be clear about what you would want an assistant to do. For example they could

- help the child to access the curriculum by reading text or scribing
- enable work in a small group
- enable practical activities in the implementation of individual literacy and numeracy programmes
- enable the child to stay on task.

Monitoring and reviewing progress

You also need to comment on how the child's progress will be reviewed and monitored. It's usually sufficient to undertake to review termly, in liaison with parents and other agencies.

From draft to final statement

Once the LEA has received information from all those involved with the child, an LEA officer draws up a draft statement. This is then circulated to all those who contributed in order to ensure that their intentions have been met. At this stage, Part 4 of the document is left blank. This is the section that names a particular school. The LEA is not able to compel a school to take a child. However, neither is the school able to refuse a child simply because they feel unable to cater for their needs. The Disability Act Part 4, 2002, has strengthened the rights of children to attend their local mainstream schools. To all intents and purposes, schools are required to take in children whatever their needs. The onus is on the school to adapt to the child, rather than send the child elsewhere.

The LEA will send the draft statement to an appropriate school, often the school the child attends. The school then has a period of time to consider whether or not they can meet the needs of the child, or what accommodations they would need to make in order to do so. If there are no disagreements, the statement is issued as a final statement.

Statutory review meetings

Statutory review meetings are formal occasions when a child's statement is reviewed. You have to take care that you follow all the correct procedures and you will find guidelines on this in The Code of Practice. You should also have guidance from your own local authority on their preferred procedures for what happens at these meetings.

Preparing for the meeting

In principle there should be a review of a child's statement at least once a year, usually around the time of the original statement. Check the date at the end of the statement to find out when it was issued. Then try to set the date so that the meeting and the paperwork can be completed by this day in the following year.

Sometimes reviews have to be conducted less than a year after the date of the statement or the previous review. This might be specified in the statement, it might be brought about by changing circumstances or it might be because the child is due to transfer schools or move on to the next stage of their education.

If the child is due to transfer to their next school, try to hold the meeting as early as possible in the school year. If the parents have made a decision about their preferred choice of school, you can then invite the SEN coordinator or the headteacher from that school to attend the meeting. She or he will then be able to decide whether to accept the child and, if they do, to carry out practical modifications to the school that may be needed and to consider appointing suitable support staff.

Your local authority may send you reminders of review meetings needed each term, or a list of dates at the beginning of the school year. On receipt of this information, plan the dates and put them in the school diary. If the LEA doesn't send reminders as a matter of course, this is a job you should do at the start of the school year. They should be noted on your SEN Development Plan (see page 29).

Statutory review schedule

- **Beginning of year** – set dates for the year.
- **Six weeks prior to the meeting** – send out invitations and requests for reports if necessary.
- **Two weeks prior to the meeting** – send out copies of the reports.
- **One week after the meeting** – send out minutes, any additional reports to absentees and a copy of the statement marked with any recommended amendments to the LEA officer for SEN.

The people who should be invited to attend the meeting will vary, depending on the special needs of the child and the guidance from your local authority. In general you need to invite

- the LEA education officer for special needs
- the child's parents
- the educational psychologist
- the headteacher
- the class teacher
- the teaching assistant
- any other professional involved in the original statement and any person involved with the child since the statement, such as a speech and language therapist, a physiotherapist, an occupational therapist or a social worker

- any specialist teacher from the authority's support staff, such as a teacher of the deaf, a teacher for the visually impaired, a specific learning difficulties teacher or a teacher for children with emotional and behavioural difficulties.

Parents have an important part to play in reviews but they don't always feel able to participate fully, being surrounded by professionals. You can help them to feel relaxed by making sure that they understand why the review is being held, what will happen and what the possible outcomes might be.

Children's own views should also be taken into account – even if they are not always easy to gather and interpret. Parents will be able to tell you something about what their child feels and wants, but you can also contribute by talking with the child and making a note of what he or she says. If appropriate you could ask the child to write something that you can then take to the meeting.

You need to invite people to attend the meeting at least six weeks in advance. Some professionals may attend reviews for more than one child in your school. If it's possible to arrange two or even three meetings on one day this will help them to use their time efficiently. You will need to send out any reports two weeks before the review date so that everyone has time to read them.

Holding the meeting

The meeting will usually take between one and two hours, so you need to think carefully about an appropriate space in your school. People need to be seated comfortably with a table for papers. Try to make sure that you won't be disturbed. If you have to use the staffroom, make sure that the staff know well in advance that they won't be able to get in there for that period of time and that they will need to make alternative arrangements for breaks.

If you plan your agenda well it will be a helpful guide to writing up the report at the close of the meeting. Print enough copies so that each person can have their own copy. Have your own copy printed with large spaces after each item so that you can make notes.

Check with the recommendations from your local authority for any additional information they require on the forms you return to them. Add these into the agenda at an appropriate place.

Agenda for annual review of a statement

1 Welcome and introductions

2 Apologies for absence

3 Reports (list, by designation, all those who replied that they would send or bring a report)

4 The child's views

5 Changes in need since the last meeting

6 Current provision

7 Recommended changes to provision

8 Does the statement need to be maintained?

9 Recommended changes to the statement

10 Any additional comments

At the beginning of the meeting agree who will take the minutes. As SEN coordinator you are probably the best person to do this, as you will be filling in all the forms after the meeting. However, you may wish to ask somebody else to help, especially if you are also chairing the meeting.

Keep notes as the meeting progresses. You don't need to record details from the reports as you already have copies of these. Keep notes of any additional points made, such as

• concerns raised about the level or type of provision

• recommendations for necessary or desirable changes

• requests for information and how it can be gathered

• any actions identified and who has agreed to take them

• who else should be asked to do something and who is going to make the request.

Minutes should

• be clear and succinct

• include phrases such as '...was discussed', but not details of the discussion

• include recommendations made

• include actions to be taken and the name of the person who has agreed to undertake them.

Check that the minutes are an accurate reflection of the meeting. Send copies to all those who attended and those who were invited but were unable to attend. These people also need copies of any reports that were not sent before the meeting. Remember to put a copy of everything into the child's file.

Follow-up

After the meeting you need to carry out a number of tasks.

• Make sure that the minutes are distributed to every person invited to attend. If any reports were not sent in beforehand, make sure that those people who were unable to attend the meeting receive copies.

• Make sure that any changes to be made to the statement are clearly marked and sent to the appropriate person within your local authority.

• Set up a meeting to write the next IEP bearing in mind the recommendations of the meeting.

• Talk with the parents and the child about what has happened and what will happen next.

Child protection case conferences

A child protection case conference is called when there is concern about a child suffering or likely to suffer from significant harm. Social services arrange the meeting, but any professional who is concerned about a child can ask for a conference to be called. The headteacher is usually the school's named person for child protection, but as SEN coordinator you may be asked to take on this role and thus will be invited to represent the school at these conferences.

Your attendance at the meeting is important because you see the child more often than any of the other professionals involved. You are more likely to notice

• changes in mood and behaviour

• patterns of behaviour

• changes in quality or quantity of work

• poor concentration

• changes in appearance

• differences in relationships with friends

• differences in contacts with parents or carers.

The child's work can also give you an insight into how the child is feeling. This can be noticed in drawings, drama, writing and creative play.

When attending conferences, one of the things all SEN coordinators worry about, apart from the welfare of the child, is their relationship with the parents and family. We work hard to develop a relationship and a sense of trust. This can require a lot of time and effort and one thing we fear is this trust being lost through the conference. However, a large number of parents seem to be quite relieved that the difficulties they have in bringing up their child are being recognised.

This is particularly so if the outcome of the conference gives them support and it can in fact increase the trust between the parents and the school. The greater understanding you gain of the background to the child's home and family, the more this can be beneficial to your work with the parents.

Before you go, a report needs to be sent to the chairperson, at least 48 hours before the meeting. Do be aware that this report will be shared with the parents. The report should have details of the child's progress, behaviour and attendance. Other information may be useful, such as the child's appearance and relationships with other children and adults. Some authorities produce a form that outlines areas that they want information on.

Writing a case report

When completing the report, remember that the information given should be factual. Don't repeat hearsay – if anybody at the meeting challenges your report, you want to be certain that you can support what you've said. When referring to the appearance of the child, use words like 'appears to be' or 'seems', eg. 'he often appears to be tired'.

When you go to case conferences, you need to take evidence that will support the written report and any notes that may have been made about the child's welfare. Copies of all reports submitted to the chair will be circulated at the meeting. However, it's also worth taking a copy of your own report, as paperwork can sometimes go astray. Don't feel you've got to take bundles of papers, but evidence that may be useful could include

- attendance records, including details of arriving late for school and/or unaccounted absences
- records of the child not being collected from school on time, or of there being no arrangements made for the child to go home
- behaviour records
- evidence of patterns of behaviour, eg. is it often on Mondays or Fridays that incidences of challenging behaviour occur?
- details of the type of communication you've had with the parents and how often
- school achievement levels if relevant, eg. if the child is not achieving as well as you would expect.

At the conference, both professionals and family members discuss the information provided and decide whether to place the child's name on the child protection register. All the key people involved with

the child and the family will have been invited to attend. The number of people at the conference can vary considerably. As well as the chair of the meeting, a clerk, the social worker and representatives from all schools involved with children in the family, other people who may attend include

- the police
- health professionals – the GP, school medical officer, paediatrician, school nurse, health visitor
- an education welfare officer
- a solicitor
- other members of the social services, eg. family centre workers
- members of the family.

The child may be present, but this is unusual if they are under 12 years old.

There is no set seating plan, although the social worker will usually sit with the family. You will be given a copy of all the reports, including one from the social worker. This report will be detailed and contain a lot of information from the family and will give the background to the calling of the conference.

You will find that the family and social worker are not in the room initially. This is because it's normal practice for the social worker to go through their report with the family separately. The chair may also take this time to explain to the family what will happen at the meeting. There are times when confidential information will be discussed without the family being present. This may happen if there is an ongoing police investigation, or medical information that cannot be shared with all of the family.

At the beginning of the conference the chairperson will ask everybody to introduce themselves – sometimes there are name plates. It is then usual for the social worker to go through their report. There is an opportunity for everyone to ask questions. Various discussions will take place about different aspects of the report.

Other reports will be discussed and questioned. You will be asked to go through your report. This is where your evidence may be useful, but only refer to it if you are asked a specific question – remember, it's only there to back you up if necessary.

After the reports have been discussed and any other issues raised by members of the conference have been considered, the chair will summarise what has happened so far. The conference will then need to decide on the outcome.

There are three possible outcomes of a case conference.

1 There is not sufficient concern for the child to be placed on the child protection register.

2 The name of a child already on the register should be removed as there are no longer significant concerns.

3 The child's name should be placed on the register.

If a child's name is to go onto the register, then it must be decided under which category this will be. The categories are

- physical abuse

- emotional abuse

- sexual abuse

- neglect.

The conference may decide to register the child for a combination of categories – for example, neglect and physical abuse.

The chairperson will give guidance to the meeting about the category or categories under which the child will be placed on the child protection register. Each person will then be asked if they agree or disagree. The family doesn't have a say at this point.

Once it is decided to place the child's name on the child protection register, other decisions will also be made. These decisions will include how the family can be supported and so help in the protection of the child as part of the child protection plan.

The child protection plan

The plan details what needs to be done to ensure the safety of the child. A date will be set for the review conference, which should be held within three months.

When a child's name is placed on the register, a core group is formed. This group will be made up of the key professionals working with the child.

A typical core-group will consist of

- social worker

- school representative

- family.

The role of the group is to work together to put the child protection plan into action.

In the majority of cases the child will continue to live at home. If it is decided that this is not for the best then legal action will begin so that they can be taken into the care of social services.

⚠ Confidentiality

It cannot be stressed too strongly that any information you hear or read at a child protection conference is strictly confidential. All conference minutes and other records about child protection should be locked away separately from other school records.

At the meeting you will hear a lot of sensitive information about the family. It will be information that you would not usually hear and it will not just relate to the child. Some of the information will relate to other children in the family and to other family members including parents.

What you hear can sometimes be quite distressing and you will need to give yourself time to unwind after the meeting.

Your headteacher will have access to the child protection records, so you may find it useful to discuss it all with him or her.

Following the case conference

All information that you gain at the conference should be sensitively handled. Staff cannot be given the reports or minutes to read. They should be given as much information as they need to ensure the child's safety and protection. This will include anything that may contribute to the improved pastoral care of the child.

The main adults who deal with parents will need to be aware of any restrictions about access to the child by individuals or families.

Remember that the purpose of the conference is to benefit the child. So how can we ensure that at school the child does benefit from the meeting? The records that you used to write your report may come in useful now. The evidence may show that Monday mornings are a particularly difficult time for the child – for instance, they display challenging behaviour. In the light of what you now know about the child's home life, are there strategies that could be adopted to ease them into school life? The following are some strategies to consider.

- They may need some time to sit quietly.

- A book to write or draw in can be helpful – this is a book for the child only, and not for anyone else to see.

- You may want to ask them if there is anyone that they would like to talk to when they feel the need to talk.

- It may not be practical for the child to complete homework at home. Is there a way that the school can give any help with this? Lunchtime or after-school homework clubs may be possible.

- Is the child often late for school? If your school has a policy of children who are late going to the school office when they arrive, perhaps another child from the class could go and meet them. This will help to alleviate the unease of walking into a class where everyone else is settled.

- Not having a school uniform can be uncomfortable for the child and beyond their control. Strategies to make this easier could be to have a spare school sweatshirt that they know is available.

Above all, don't make a big issue of it. Don't forget that the child will already be feeling different and may not want too much 'special' attention. There are some children who like to talk to their classmates about what's happening to them, but this must be their choice. By using some of these strategies you're being sympathetic to the needs of all the children.

Finally

The role of SEN coordinator may seem overwhelming at times, but while it has its challenging moments, it can also be very rewarding. It is important to remember that provision for children with special educational needs is a matter for the school as a whole. You are part of a team who, together, can change children's lives for the better.

References

DfES (2001) *Special Educational Needs Code of Practice.* Ref: 581/2001. London: DfES.

DfEE (2000) *Professional Development Support for Teaching and Learning – consultation document.* Ref: 0008/2000. London: DfEE.

Teacher Training Association (1998) *National Standards for Special Educational Needs Coordinators.* London: TTA.

Thanks to Ann Berger, Lynn Cousins, Sue Dow, Fiona Gibson, Beth Huke and Graham Reeves for their contributions to this chapter.

Advice from the school towards a statement

If the LEA agrees to a statutory assessment they will request an assessment from the school. This two-page prompt sheet will help you to provide the information required to give a complete picture of the child within your school setting.

General

- Does the child usually enjoy school?
- What sort of relationships do they have with adults and with their peers?
- Do they seem aware of the purpose of school, and realise that it's about learning?
- Which activities do they enjoy and what activities are they good at?

Attendance

- Is the child at school regularly and on time?
- If not, what are the reasons for this?
- What has the school done to change the situation?

Access to the curriculum

- Is the child able to listen and concentrate during whole-class sessions?
- Can they manage this when working in a small group or with a partner or support staff?
- If they are not able to sustain concentration, what do they do?
- Do they need tasks explained and demonstrated before they are able to attempt them?
- Is the curriculum that the rest of the class is receiving appropriate for them?
- How do they approach directed tasks?
- Are they able to retain information, or to generalise their knowledge?
- Do they have the vocabulary to explain and describe what they are doing or their difficulties?
- Are there any other speech-related difficulties?

Confidence and the ability to work independently

- Is the child willing to attempt whatever is asked of them?
- Are they able to sustain concentration and complete tasks?
- Will they persist at a task in order to complete it, or are they likely to give up or ask for help?
- Are they able to attempt tasks before asking for help?
- Are there any particular areas where they are able to work independently, such as practical activities, or where there are real materials to work with?
- How do they respond to written tasks, books or number activities?
- How do they respond to adult support?
- Are they able to offer their ideas and opinions in a whole-class or group situation?
- If they are not able to do it alone, will they do it with support and encouragement?

Social skills

- Does the child have friends within the class or the wider school community?
- Do they interact with their peers on an equal basis?
- Are they able to initiate play or communications with others?
- If other children are hurt or upset by the child, do they understand the part they have played in this?

Physical skills

- Does the child have age-appropriate coordination and spatial awareness?
- For an older child, does the work that is put down on paper reflect their oral ability?

Specific needs

You will also need to think about specific needs or areas of difficulty and what stage the child is at in building up skills and concepts. It's useful to describe these in terms of steps that need to be achieved and/or as objectives that the child needs to be working on. You also need to include any resources that are important in supporting and sustaining learning.

Some examples are given in the box below.

Is the child able to remember what has been learned previously?	Needs to develop memory.
Are they able to apply their knowledge to a new situation? eg. if they can read words within a favourite story, do they recognise those words when they encounter them in other places?	Needs to learn in small, sequential steps, building on previous knowledge, with plenty of opportunity to consolidate what they have learned. Needs opportunities to see a task demonstrated and then to watch others completing it, before attempting it themselves.
Does the child have any sight vocabulary?	Needs to develop a sight vocabulary for writing.
Do they misread or misunderstand social situations?	Needs to practise social skills and rehearse responses to problems.

These are some of the areas to think about.

Literacy

- Does the child have a vocabulary of words that they are able to read? Are they also able to write these words?
- Do they have the phonic skills to attempt unknown words?
- Do they need support to read texts and to access the curriculum?

Maths

- Does the child understand the concepts of addition, subtraction, multiplication and division?
- Do they have immediate recall of basic number bonds and tables?

Behaviour and social skills

- Is the child able to manage boundaries set by adults?
- Are they unpredictable under certain circumstances?
- Are they able to cooperate with other children?

CHAPTER 2
Plan, do, review

Planning is an important part of the SEN coordinator's role. Very little can be achieved if SEN issues are not viewed as a whole-school responsibility and therefore part of the whole school's forward planning. The 2001 SEN Code of Practice emphasises that '...all teachers are teachers of SEN children'. An SEN coordinator needs to be proactive in identifying not only the short-term, but also the medium- and long-term needs of both the children and the staff. In this way you can ensure that you offer effective, ongoing SEN provision, rather than just reacting to short-term needs.

The Code also recognises the tremendous responsibility that SEN coordinators have and recommends that they should not only be given sufficient time to fulfil their responsibilities but should also be given status by being part of the senior management team. In this way an SEN coordinator can become more involved in forward planning, and SEN provision is accepted as an integral part of planning for the whole school. The National Standards for SEN Coordinators describe seven key outcomes of SEN coordination. One of these states that effective coordination of SEN results in

> '...headteachers and other senior managers who recognise that the curriculum must be relevant to all pupils by taking SEN into account in the formulation and implementation of policies throughout the school; understand how best to support those with responsibility for SEN coordination...' (TTA, 1998 – 2e)

This chapter looks at the cycle of planning, acting upon the plans, and then reviewing the action taken in order to inform the next stage of planning. In your role as SEN coordinator you will have the opportunity to work with colleagues on different types of planning documents. These documents all have a part to play in ensuring that effective provision is made for all children including those with special educational needs.

For each type of planning document we have provided an example of a completed sheet. Blank grids can be found at the end of this chapter on pages 39–43.

School improvement plan

The school improvement plan (or school development plan) highlights the action points that have been identified to aid school improvement. This plan is usually compiled by the headteacher, governors and senior management team after consultation with other members of staff. It covers a number of areas, including

- **curriculum** – subject and policy reviews, action plans, assessment, monitoring and reporting arrangements, resource needs and other issues
- **finance** – budget preparation, school fund audit, policy and financial management review
- **staffing** – performance management, review of job descriptions, staff development and training needs, recruitment
- **general purposes** – school buildings and grounds improvements and maintenance, site security, health and safety, equipment and furniture needs, the school prospectus.

Other areas may be covered in the school improvement plan, depending on the particular needs identified in the school. The SEN needs identified should be clarified in the SEN development plan or action plan. It is important for the school improvement plan to be a progressive and flexible document in order to support school improvement at all levels. Some areas identified may require a longer period of time to implement, while others may need to be reviewed in the light of new directives from the government.

Example

On the sample plan shown it can be seen clearly that the curriculum focus for the autumn term was on English and maths. Action plans for both of these subject areas were to be completed from the previous term with additional details. The main aim was to provide motivation for the improvement of the children's writing skills. Analysis of the Key Stage 2 National Curriculum test results had indicated that most children were achieving better results in reading

School improvement plan

Objective	Action	Personnel	Timescale	Resourcing	Success criteria
English/Literacy Action Plan	Complete new Literacy Action Plan to include • modelled writing • activities to teach transfer and generalisation of grammar skills • differentiation in literacy planning • able children – extension and enrichment activities • develop alternative methods of recording	Literacy coordinator, SEN coordinator	Sept 2002	Meeting time	Plan completed in consultation with the SEN coordinator, monitoring and actions taking place leading to improvement in standards
Maths/Numeracy Action Plan	Complete new Numeracy Action Plan to include • organisation and use of new resources • differentiation in numeracy planning • able children – extension and enrichment activities • develop alternative methods of recording	Numeracy coordinator, SEN coordinator	Sept 2002	Meeting time	Plan completed in consultation with the SEN coordinator, monitoring and actions taking place leading to improvement in standards
Staff Training (SEN)	SEN coordinator to deliver training on the use of alternative methods of recording	Teaching staff, TAs	Oct 2002	2 x 1 hour 2 x 1 hour	Children to feel more confident with recording, links to IEP targets
INSET	LEA advisor to deliver ICT INSET on using ICT to stimulate and support the development of writing skills	Teaching staff, TAs	Nov 2002	INSET day for all staff	Staff to feel confident, improved motivation for writing, children's writing skills enhanced

than in writing. All staff agreed that motivation was a key factor and that a large number of children in the school were motivated to write when they were given opportunities to use alternative methods of recording, rather than just narrative writing. The staff wanted to develop teaching skills that would enhance the children's ability to write successfully using a variety of formats.

The literacy and numeracy action plans were implemented at the beginning of term and staff were asked to share their successful ideas for the transfer and generalisation of grammar skills. Many of these ideas proved to be practical and fun. A bank of ideas was compiled for each year group. In this way the children began to see that grammar skills could be used in a range of contexts. By sharing ideas, the educational needs of all the children were recognised and the SEN coordinator was able to show how some of the ideas could be incorporated into IEPs.

The decision to ensure that differentiated activities were shown on both literacy and numeracy plans proved to be quite difficult for those class teachers who had a number of children needing a high level of support. Nevertheless, everyone agreed that three levels of differentiation should be shown on both literacy and numeracy plans.

Staff training in the use of alternative methods of recording was organised and delivered by the SEN coordinator (see SEN development plan, below). The ICT INSET day was organised and delivered by an advisory teacher and the staff were introduced to a number of programs designed to stimulate children's writing.

All the actions undertaken from the school improvement plan were monitored by the senior management team and carefully evaluated at staff meetings by all the teaching staff. It was agreed that the sharing of good ideas had been very successful and should be applied in other areas of literacy and numeracy on a regular basis. The ICT INSET day had been a helpful introduction to using ICT as a stimulus for developing children's writing skills, but the deployment of computers in the school needed to be considered in order to make the best use of some of the programs. Most staff felt that they needed more support with ideas for differentiation in both literacy and numeracy. It was decided that planning for differentiation should be a focus for future staff meetings, with the SEN coordinator taking a leading role.

The senior management team reviewed the curriculum focus of the school improvement plan at the end of the term. The success criteria formed the basis for their review. It was decided that some areas of the literacy and numeracy action plans needed additional input and should be monitored during the following term. The SEN coordinator was asked to monitor the use of alternative methods of recording (see SEN development plan, below) and suggest classroom organisation strategies.

SEN development or action plan

The SEN development plan should be linked to the school improvement plan. It should clarify whole-school SEN issues and show how these connect with specific areas of SEN in the school. It should also detail the key areas of action for each term and chart SEN development in the school for the year. All senior management staff should be given a copy of the SEN development plan. It is also a good idea to have a copy displayed, so that other staff have an overview of SEN development and are aware of the timescales for the introduction of SEN initiatives.

As SEN coordinator, and a member of the senior management team, you will be able to link the needs of individual children and staff to the 'big picture' of whole-school improvement. Your role as coordinator of SEN provision gives you the opportunity to monitor SEN issues on a regular basis, and this, in turn, guides your contribution to the school improvement plan and some areas of the SEN development plan. The key areas in your SEN development plan may include

- **curriculum** – subject and policy action plans, review of curriculum planning and differentiation arrangements, resource needs and other issues, assessment, monitoring and reviewing arrangements for children on School Action, School Action Plus and for those who have a statement of special educational need.

- **staff training** – organise training for all staff as identified in the school improvement plan, as well as specific individual training identified through performance management reviews

- **external agencies** – liaison meetings, assessment and review meetings, consultation meetings and review of specific staff INSET needs

- **finance** – review of staffing and resources needed to support the children identified at School Action and School Action Plus and those who are statemented.

Other areas may be covered in your SEN development plan, depending on the particular needs identified in your school. However, an effective SEN development plan should ensure that

- children are given opportunities to make progress towards targets set in their IEPs through the provision of appropriate planning and differentiation arrangements
- teachers are familiar with, and able to incorporate, SEN strategies for learning into their lessons
- teachers receive training on new SEN initiatives and feel confident to implement them with the support of the SEN coordinator
- parents are viewed as partners in the education process
- both the headteacher and the SEN governor have an active part to play in the development of SEN provision in the school
- Teaching assistants are trained to undertake the duties required of them and supported by the SEN coordinator and the class teacher in carrying out these duties
- external specialists are aware of SEN issues in the school and can offer support and training as appropriate.

Staff training needs to be planned to ensure that

- children are supported by teaching staff who are trained to understand and meet most of their needs within the context of the classroom
- children are supported by teaching assistants who are trained to understand and meet some of their specific needs within the context of differentiated groupings
- children have continuity of support when teaching assistants are absent
- both children and parents feel confident that school staff understand their needs.

Example

The sample plan shows that the SEN curriculum focus for the autumn term was linked clearly to the school improvement plan. The SEN development plan also outlines the systems available for regular monitoring and review of SEN provision in the school. Although the Code of Practice does not require a special needs register of children to be kept, nevertheless, it is important that teachers in each year group have, at the beginning of the school year, a list of children who have been identified as having special educational needs. It is helpful if individual learning difficulties are highlighted and support strategies suggested (see Chapter 4: Strategies for learning).

The multi-professional consultation meeting provided a forum for discussing individual children's needs, arranging dates for attendance at annual reviews, discussing whole-school SEN issues and organising support and training from external specialists during the year. Some of the specialists were able to provide the SEN coordinator with materials to support staff training on the use of alternative methods of recording. These included mind-maps, writing frames, flow charts, diagrams, comic strip stories and posters.

As SEN coordinator, you were asked to provide training for all staff, including teaching assistants, on the use of alternative methods of recording. The teaching assistant training was incorporated into the school day and consisted of two one-hour afternoon sessions. The teacher training consisted of two one-hour sessions during staff meetings. A range of formats for recording information were presented in a practical way, and staff were guided into choosing the most suitable formats to use with children who had particular learning difficulties. The action, timescale, resourcing and success criteria for this training were noted on your SEN development plan.

As part of the senior management team, you were asked to monitor differentiation for children with learning difficulties in both literacy and numeracy. This involved giving class teachers support with planning, deployment of teaching assistants, grouping and teaching strategies. It also involved making formal and informal classroom observations.

All the actions undertaken, with all the staff, from the SEN development plan were monitored by the senior management team and carefully evaluated at staff meetings by all the teaching staff. It was felt that the use of alternative methods of recording was helpful to those children who had difficulty with sustaining a piece of narrative writing, but it should not be used as an alternative to narrative writing. It was pointed out that there were opportunities to use different writing formats in other areas of the curriculum as well as in the literacy and numeracy hours. It was decided that all children should produce an agreed number of pieces of narrative and non-narrative writing each term and that these should be linked to their personal targets for writing.

You were asked to monitor the use of alternative methods of recording for individual children and guide teachers into using the most suitable formats for specific children. You were also asked to advise on classroom organisation strategies and groupings. Most

SEN development plan

Objective	Action	Personnel	Timescale	Resourcing	Success criteria
Multi-professional consultation meeting	Prepare agenda for meeting between educational psychologist, speech and language therapist, learning support services and other external agencies	Headteacher, SEN coordinator, EP, SLT, LSS and other agencies	Sept 2002	Meeting time	SEN issues addressed, dates for staff training and individual consultation times arranged
LEA reviews for children transferring to secondary school	Plan timetable of visits from educational psychologist and arrange meetings with parents, collect information for staff and parents	SEN coordinator, (primary and secondary), parents, class teacher, external agencies	throughout the term	Liaison/ meeting time	Annual reviews completed
Complete lists of children receiving SEN provision for each year group	List children in each year group and detail individual learning difficulties	SEN coordinator	Sept 2002	Meeting time	Up to date lists available for reference
Complete new Literacy Action Plan	SEN coordinator to liaise with literacy coordinator to write and monitor literacy action plan (see school improvement plan)	Literacy coordinator, SEN coordinator	Sept 2002	Meeting time	Plans completed, actions and monitoring taking place, improvement in literacy standards
Complete new Numeracy Action Plan	SEN coordinator to liaise with numeracy coordinator to write and monitor numeracy action plan (see school improvement plan)	Numeracy coordinator, SEN coordinator	Sept 2002	Meeting time	Plans completed, actions and monitoring taking place, improvement in numeracy standards
Staff training	SEN coordinator to deliver training on the use of alternative methods of recording	SEN coordinator, all staff	Oct 2002	4 x 1 hour	Children more confident with recording, enhanced writing skills

staff felt that they needed more support with ideas for differentiation in both literacy and numeracy. It was decided that planning for differentiation should be a focus for future staff meetings with you, as SEN coordinator, taking a leading role.

When undertaking a review of the SEN development plan at the end of each term it is a good idea to organise a meeting with the headteacher and SEN governor in order to share successes and address difficulties.

INSET plan

INSET plans need to be linked closely to individual performance management targets, as well as to the whole-school needs that have been highlighted in the school improvement plan. However, only a few performance management targets will relate to specific SEN issues. As SEN coordinator, you need to ensure that SEN INSET is relevant and meets the needs of children, staff and parents. Some specific training, such as learning sign language, may be better delivered to small groups on a weekly basis. Other SEN issues need to be discussed by all the staff together. The staff training relating to SEN, that has been highlighted in the school improvement plan and clarified in the SEN development plan, needs to be incorporated into the INSET programme. It may be delivered via

- INSET days centred on national or international guest speakers
- INSET days organised and delivered by you and other SEN professionals
- twilight sessions related to specific training
- staff meetings that focus on specific issues, eg. alternative methods of recording
- LEA-accredited and non-accredited courses
- government-funded courses.

INSET days usually need to be planned well in advance, particularly if they are to be delivered by high-profile guest speakers. These days usually focus on specific teaching and learning issues, new government initiatives or an area of the curriculum. Many of these days are organised by the LEA, professional bodies or clusters of schools in order to minimise the cost to individual schools. You may be asked to organise an INSET day for your school on a specific SEN issue that has been highlighted in the school improvement plan. You will need to contact any specialists or LEA advisers to help you deliver the INSET. Formal consultation meetings with professional and LEA advisers usually focus on whole

school SEN issues, as well as individual children's needs. During these meetings it is important that they are made aware of any staff training needs. Twilight sessions relating to specific training (eg. strategies for working with children who have Autistic Spectrum disorder) can be organised. LEA advisers can also give advice on the suitability of certain courses for different members of staff.

The INSET plan is only part of the training programme for the year. Many staff attend both accredited and non-accredited courses related to their curriculum responsibilities and to their individual performance management targets. The INSET plan acts as a framework for school improvement and staff training. In order to be effective, SEN training needs to complement whole-school INSET, as well as providing opportunities for learning about specific disorders and conditions. For example, during an INSET day on science, teachers could be reminded about using alternative methods of recording for children who have difficulty with writing. An SEN coordinator should remember that a busy teacher, with a large class of mixed ability children, needs to be shown practical support strategies that are manageable within an inclusive context.

Example

INSET days were agreed in advance and linked to other staff training. Staff meetings and twilight sessions were planned on a termly basis, with one staff meeting a month being flexible in order to allow for sharing of expertise and administrative arrangements.

The INSET plan provides a good example of the 'plan, do, review' cycle. It is important that time is allocated for monitoring and reviewing the actions taken after any INSET. In this way everyone is contributing to school improvement.

As can be seen from the sample INSET plan the first group of staff meetings in September encouraged staff to take a close look at the way in which writing was presented to the children of all abilities in the school. These initial meetings asked the question 'Where are we now?' The next group of staff meetings looked at some strategies to improve motivation for writing. This gave everyone an opportunity to explore different ways of presenting writing as an exciting and interesting activity. The INSET day on using ICT for developing writing skills showed the staff some programs that would challenge the children's writing abilities at all levels. By using these programs with the children, staff were able to identify individual learning styles (see Chapter 4:

INSET plan

	Sept	Oct	Nov	Dec	Jan	Feb	March	April	May	June	July
1			INSET – using ICT for writing			INSET – teaching and learning styles	INSET – focus on science			INSET – compiling subject portfolios of children's work	INSET – creating a dyslexia-friendly school
2	Staff meeting – narrative writing	Staff meeting – focus on grammar activities	Staff meeting – evaluation of ICT INSET	Staff meeting – circletime							
3	Staff meeting – writing resources	Staff meeting – alternative methods of recording	Staff meeting – evaluation of methods of recording	Staff meeting – managing challenging behaviour							
4	Staff meeting – extension writing for able children	Staff meeting – alternative methods of recording									
5			Twilight session – classroom organisation and grouping		Twilight session – differentiation in the literacy hour						
6											

Strategies for Learning) and chart progress. All the teachers were keen to develop the use of ICT for writing and asked the SEN coordinator to advise them on the most suitable programs for particular children.

When reviewing the use of alternative methods of recording, most staff felt that they needed more guidance from the SEN coordinator about choosing the most suitable formats to use with children who had particular learning difficulties. Although this was outlined during the training sessions, it was felt that more specific guidance was needed. Similarly, staff also felt that they needed more specific guidance with regard to ICT programs and children with special needs. However, the main outcome of the ICT action review was the decision that ICT resources needed to be grouped and shared more often so that the children could use the computers for writing more frequently.

The review part of the cycle was an essential element. It provided information for further staff training needs and these were built into the plan for the following term. Although INSET days needed to be planned for the year, staff training sessions were more flexible and could be the direct result of the 'plan, do, review' cycle.

The SEN coordinator plays an important part in the INSET plan. Even when the focus does not appear to have a particular special needs connection, staff often require guidance on how to adapt ideas to make them relevant to special needs children. You need to be able to organise training for staff on SEN issues but, most importantly, also have to be able to guide and advise across a range of contexts. This, in itself, is a form of INSET. Sometimes, those unplanned moments are the most useful.

Individual education plan

An individual education plan (IEP) is a record of the targets and strategies that have been employed to enable a child to make progress. It is an important document because it charts the response that the school has made to the special educational needs of an individual child and provides evidence of the nature of any intervention. It is essential that the 'plan, do, review' cycle is used, as this enables everyone, including the child, to recognise success and identify 'next step' targets.

The SEN Code of Practice states that IEPs should focus only on what is additional to and different from the basic school entitlement offered to all children.

It suggests that the SEN coordinator should liaise with parents, staff and children to plan and implement an IEP. The IEP should

- include three or four individual short-term targets that match the child's needs
- be reviewed at least every six months, preferably every term
- outline teaching strategies to be used, as well as resources (both human and materials).

It is also important that IEPs are working documents and that targets relate to the school curriculum as much as possible. In order to do this, the SEN coordinator, the class teacher, the teaching assistant and the parents need to identify the difficulties encountered by the child, within the classroom, and then investigate strategies for intervention that support class-based learning. However, some children may need the support of more specific teaching strategies. When these are needed, it is important to remember that the skills should be taught within a range of contexts, so that the children are able to transfer their learning from one context to another and not see them as isolated skills.

IEPs should be shared with the parents and the children when appropriate. 'Practitioners should ensure that where an Individual Education Plan (IEP) is developed the child is involved at an appropriate level.' (DfES, 2001 – 3:7).

Most children like to feel that they own the targets that are set and are more willing to work towards them if they are part of the target setting process.

'IEPs should include information about
- the short-term targets set for or by the child
- the teaching strategies to be used
- the provision to be put in place
- when the plan is to be reviewed
- success and/or exit criteria
- outcomes (to be recorded when the IEP is reviewed).'
DfES, 2001 – 5:50)

IEPs provide a focus for good practice and encourage you and class teachers to investigate a range of strategies for learning. The writing, monitoring and reviewing of an IEP, although time consuming, provides the SEN coordinator with opportunities to interact with parents, teachers, teaching assistants and sometimes external agencies. In this way you can be proactive in developing collaborative educational effort as all those involved with the child work together to support his or her special educational needs.

Individual education plan

Name: J. S.   **Response:** School Action Plus   **Year:** 5

Review (Dec 2002)

J has made good progress with her reading skills and continues to be successful in role-play and drama activities. She continues to have difficulty sustaining attention, though there has been some improvement when she is working in a small guided reading or writing group. She does need constant reminders to stay on task and works better when she has short, clearly defined targets set for each part of the lesson. J's ability to sustain attention is affected by her restricted auditory memory. She now has a diagnosis of Developmental Coordination Disorder from the occupational therapist. J has made steady progress with her ability to understand and recall vocabulary though she continues to need to develop her awareness of the relationships between words (categories, functions, attributes). She has difficulty with using some correct verb tenses and prepositions and needs the support of visual material to remind her. J enjoys using ICT as a learning tool and has expressed her wish to improve her keyboard skills as she would like to be able to type rather than write. She also needs to use alternative methods of recording more independently in some areas of the curriculum. J's parents are keen for her to develop these skills in preparation for her transfer to secondary education in a year's time.

Concerns

J continues to have difficulties with

- receptive language skills
- listening and attention skills
- restricted auditory memory
- gross and fine motor skills

Targets for Jan 2003	Strategies and resources	Success criteria
Use correct verb tense in both oral and written language (high- and medium-frequency verbs – lists 1 and 2 in National Literacy Strategy).	Individual and group activities using Colorcards (Winslow) Guided reading and writing activities Programme of activities set by the speech and language therapist for parents to implement.	Begin to use correct verb tense in all high-frequency verbs and some medium-frequency verbs (oral and written).
Develop keyboard skills to Level 2.	Programme taught and monitored by LSA twice a week.	Able to compose written work on the computer.
Develop gross and fine motor skills.	Programme set by occupational therapist, implemented by LSA 3 x 20 mins per week.	Improved coordination skills.
Use alternative methods of recording more independently.	Mind maps, flow charts, diagrams, writing frames, comic strip stories.	Able to use these methods after initial adult input.

Monday	Tuesday	Wednesday	Thursday	Friday
Language activities with MS	In class support HL		In class support HL	
		Language activities with MS		In class support HL
OT activities with RM	OT activities with RM		OT activities with RM	
				Keyboard skills with ND
		Keyboard skills with ND		

The example IEP shown on page 35 was reviewed with both parents and the child. It shows how a graduated response to the child's needs has involved a number of professionals at School Action Plus. As the parents became aware of the complex nature of J's difficulties during Year 3, they agreed to support her at home with developing her language skills. The speech and language therapist set a programme of activities to develop J's understanding and use of vocabulary and this was very successful. Both J and her parents were pleased with their success. They were prepared to continue working in this way to support other areas of J's language development.

The diagnosis made by the occupational therapist confirmed the SEN coordinator's views that J had some dyspraxic difficulties. As well as a programme of activities, set by the occupational therapist and taught and monitored by a teaching assistant twice a week, the class teacher undertook to incorporate some activities into PE and games sessions. Several other children in the class benefited from these activities.

Both J and her parents were apprehensive about her transfer to secondary school the following year. They were anxious to ensure that J had the skills to work more independently. The SEN coordinator suggested that J should be given the opportunity to use alternative methods of recording, where possible, as this would provide a framework for her ideas. A teaching assistant could give initial support, but gradually J should aim to work more independently. J agreed that she did tend to rely on teaching assistant support and expressed a wish to develop her keyboard skills further so that she could type out longer narrative pieces of writing.

J took an active part in the 'plan, do, review' cycle for her IEP. She was well supported by her parents at home and was becoming more aware of her strengths than of her difficulties. She had a large circle of friends and was a confident member of the class. J enjoyed taking part in drama and role play and had developed her reading skills through this area of the curriculum. She was positive about the targets set in her IEP and was confident that she could achieve the next level with her keyboard skills. She was motivated to try to become a more independent worker, with the support of alternative methods of recording.

Literacy hour plan

The planning suggested for the literacy hour in the Literacy Strategy is designed to provide more time for the teacher to interact with the children as a class.

The numeracy hour is designed in a similar way. This kind of approach requires the teacher to be highly skilled at controlled differentiation. She or he needs to be able to challenge the children at different levels when using a common theme or text.

The literacy hour allows for flexibility of content level and it is recognised that some groups of children will need to work at earlier levels than those specified in the framework for their year group. Some children will need to work on the development of particular literacy skills and often these can be incorporated into the guided group work. For example a child with dyslexic difficulties may need to work on an intensive phonological awareness programme organised by you and this could be part of a guided group session where other children in the class could benefit from the same kind of focus. teaching assistants can be trained to deliver these kinds of programmes, monitor the progress of the children and report back to the class teacher or the SEN coordinator when a child needs to take the next step.

When planning a literacy hour, the teacher will need to look through the objectives for the relevant term and focus on what they know the majority of the class can do. They may cover the range required for that year group, but realise that they need to use the objectives suggested for word level or sentence level work from an earlier term to suit the needs of the children in the class. Even when this kind of differentiation is planned, the teacher needs to challenge the children with questions at different levels of complexity, in order to ensure that all children are making progress.

The 'plan, do, review' cycle is also an important part of the literacy hour. The children will be unable to move on in literacy if the teacher does not review the progress that they have made and analyse any difficulties encountered. The older children can be encouraged to take part in the cycle by setting their own literacy targets and reviewing them termly. Children with IEPs will already be part of this process and can work towards their objectives within the context of the literacy hour. Some children may need to work on some of their objectives outside the literacy hour as well.

It is important for the self-esteem of all children that they feel that they can take an active part in literacy hour lessons, whatever their level of ability. Guided group reading and writing is an important part of the literacy hour and is the time when most special needs children feel successful. Working effectively in groups (listening to others, taking turns and sharing

Weekly literacy planning sheet

FABLES

Class: **Year:** 5 **Term:** 2

Week	Learning objectives	Whole-class shared reading and writing	Whole-class phonics, spelling, vocabulary and grammar	Guided group teaching	Independent group tasks (* shows where Js is working)	Plenary
MON	Write an alternative ending to a story. Identify and use the past tense.	Share read the story of 'The Ants and the Grasshopper'. Stop before the end and ask the children to predict the reaction of the ants.	Grammar focus – past and present tense. Remind children about the use of the past tense in stories – model examples.	Group 3 – ask children to write their own version of the end of the story (focus on use of interesting verbs)	Groups 1 and 2* – ask children to write their own version of the end of the story (focus on correct use of past tense).	Share stories. Compare with original version.
TUES	Make deductions and draw inferences from a text.	Share read the playscript 'Something to Drink'. Ask children to think about possible solutions to the crow's problem.	Phonic focus – syllable count (syllable identification in polysyllabic words).	Group 1 – reading (focus on reading playscripts with expression).	Groups 2* and 3 – in pairs, decide on a possible solution to the crow's problem and present in labelled pictorial or diagrammatic format.	Share some of the solutions. Share read the solution in the original story.
WED	Compile a word bank related to the characters in the text.	Share read the playscript 'Who Should Be King?' Ask the children to make a choice and give reasons for their choice.	Vocabulary focus – compile a personality word web for one of the birds in the playscript.	Group 2* – reading (focus on reading playscripts with expression).	Groups 1 and 3 – ask the children to compile a personality word web for one of the birds in the playscript.	Share some of the words on the word banks.
THURS	Recognise and use prepositions in context.	Share read the story of 'The Dog and his Reflection'.	Grammar focus – revise use of prepositions using visual material.	Groups 2* and 3 – reading (focus on understanding of the prepositions used in in the story).	Group 1 – reading (focus on oral syntactic cloze for prepositions linked to the story).	Ask the children to match prepositions to actions.
FRI	Recall the main points of a story. Identify syllables in polysyllabic words.	Ask the children to recall the main points of the story of 'The Dog and his Reflection'. Share write the first two sentences.	Phonic focus – syllable count (syllable identification in polysyllabic words).	Group 3 – reading (focus on reading simple playscripts with expression).	Groups 1 and 2* – ask the children to complete writing the main points of the story of 'The Dog and his Reflection' using a simple comic strip format.	Share some of the stories from each group.

37

materials) is often one of the key targets for children with specific learning difficulties. Guided group sessions give the class teacher opportunities to monitor the children's progress in these areas.

Example

Class planning involves a great deal of thought in order to meet the needs of all the children in the class. The SEN coordinator has a key role to play by suggesting appropriate activities that could be incorporated in to the literacy hour plan. Quite clearly, this does not mean that a class teacher should be managing a large number of individual tasks, as that would be impossible, and not in keeping with the focus of the literacy hour. However, it is possible to suggest curriculum-linked tasks that will support a number of children, as well as the children with IEPs. Chapter 4: Strategies for learning suggests a range of activities that could be adapted to form part of the literacy hour. It is important to remember that activities suggested for children with special needs often benefit many other children in the class, particularly visual and kinaesthetic learners.

The weekly literacy hour planning sheet shown as an example is for a class of Year 5 children. The class had a number of children who had immature language skills and needed support with word and sentence level work. Child J took an active part in all aspects of the literacy hour, but particularly enjoyed the guided group sessions, where she felt that she was working towards the targets set on her IEP. The links with her IEP can be clearly identified on the literacy plan, as follows.

- Play-reading – to develop listening and attention skills while, at the same time, giving J an opportunity to use her strengths and continue to make progress with her reading.

- Syllable count – to support J's restricted auditory memory (J had good phonic skills but was unable to recall all the sounds in longer words and this affected her spelling. She was able to identify the dominant sounds in polysyllabic words if she used syllable count as a strategy). Other children in the class had similar difficulties so this strategy was used as part of word level work.

- Past tense and preposition work linked to the texts – to support the development of J's language skills (J was able to work with a group of children who had immature language development and needed to work on similar word and sentence level targets).

- Use of diagrammatic and comic strip formats – to support more independent recording skills (the use of alternative methods of recording was a motivating factor in encouraging all the children in the class to write).

The other children in J's guided reading and writing group needed similar support, though for different reasons, and most of J's literacy targets could therefore be met in an inclusive setting.

Finally

The SEN coordinator needs to be involved in all areas of planning in the school. This does not mean that you have to produce those plans, but rather that you need to be part of a team of people who are prepared to plan for action, then monitor that action and evaluate it in order to ensure educational progress for all the children.

- The **school improvement plan** highlights the action points that have been identified to aid school improvement. As part of the senior management team, you help to compile this plan.

- The **SEN development plan** should be linked to the school improvement plan and clarify whole-school SEN issues, showing how these interact with other specific areas of SEN in the school. You have responsibility for writing this plan.

- The **INSET plan** needs to be linked closely to individual performance management targets, as well as the whole-school needs highlighted in the school improvement plan. You have both a formal and an informal role to play in this plan.

- The **IEP** should focus only on what is additional to and different from the basic school entitlement offered to all children. You act as advisor and help to write these plans.

- The **literacy hour plan** should take into account individual needs within the class and group situation when planning differentiated tasks. You need to suggest a range of activities that can be incorporated into the literacy hour.

References

DfES (2001) *Special Educational Needs Code of Practice*. Ref: 581/2001. London: DfES.

Teacher Training Association (1998) *National Standards for Special Educational Needs Coordinators*. London: TTA

School improvement plan

Objective	Action	Personnel	Timescale	Resourcing	Success criteria

SEN development plan

Objective	Action	Personnel	Timescale	Resourcing	Success criteria

INSET plan

	Sept	Oct	Nov	Dec	Jan	Feb	March	April	May	June	July	
1												
2												
3												
4												
5												
6												

Individual education plan

Name:	Response:	Year:

Review

Concerns

Targets	Strategies and resources	Success criteria

Monday	Tuesday	Wednesday	Thursday	Friday

Weekly literacy planning sheet

Class: Year: Term:

Week	Learning objectives	Whole-class shared reading and writing	Whole-class phonics, spelling, vocabulary and grammar	Guided group teaching	Independent group tasks	Plenary
MON						
TUES						
WED						
THURS						
FRI						

CHAPTER 3

Assessment

One of the common criticisms made by Ofsted is that, although schools carry out assessment, they do not analyse the assessment data sufficiently or use this data to make an impact on teaching and learning. Schools need to analyse data and act on the results, otherwise testing is pointless. Test results should have an impact on the planning of future work, in order to meet the individual needs of the children, and should result in the evaluation of teaching methods.

What is assessment?

Assessment is the gathering together of a range of information about children in order to be able to set programmes and targets for individuals or groups. To use assessment in promoting high standards, you must think about the type of data and the quantity you need to collect and methods and systems for sharing what you have found. Only collect data that will be useful to you, either to identify the problems of a named child or to look at trends within a particular class or year group, or across the school as a whole.

Consider the types of data you need to collect.

Norm-referenced data

In this type of assessment the scores are provided in norm tables that take age into account. It is useful for comparing the performance of individuals with the national average. The data is often used to record the overall performance of a child at the end of a year group and forms a summative assessment, a summing up, of the child's achievements.

Norm-referenced data is usually collected as part of whole-school assessment procedures. The type of standardised assessment that is used in your school reflects the areas of learning that have been identified for year-on-year comparison. These assessments are a useful measure of general levels of ability.

Special arrangements

As the SEN coordinator, you will often be asked by parents and teachers what can be done to help children with special educational needs who are taking end of Key Stages 1 or 2 tests, or indeed, if they have to sit the tests at all. These statutory assessment tests are intended to be suitable for the vast majority of children and it is only in very exceptional circumstances that a particular child should not take a test (or task). (The technical term for this is disapplication.) It is possible to make special arrangements, to give children with special needs equal access to the tests, but it is important that such arrangements do not give that child an unfair advantage over other children. Since special consideration can't be given during the marking of the tests, you need to look at possible arrangements before the tests are taken, keeping in mind the assessment needs of the child and your normal classroom practice.

You may need special arrangements for

• children who have a variety of special educational needs or who are undergoing statutory assessment

• children with a learning difficulty or disability likely to limit their access to the tests

• children unable to sit or work at a test for a sustained period, because of a disability or due to emotional, behavioural or social difficulties

• children with limited fluency in English, for whom English is an additional language.

The main alternatives that you can consider are

• disapplication

• early opening of the test papers

• additional time

• an adult to read the test questions/instructions (but not for English)

• an adult to scribe, or the use of ICT

• modified papers or materials

• modifications to the mental arithmetic test.

Details are set out in the QCA booklet *Assessment and Reporting Arrangements*.

Examples are

- end of Key Stage 1 tests
- end of Key Stage 2 tests
- optional National Curriculum tests
- other tests (such as reading or spelling) giving standardised scores.

Teacher assessment data

Teacher assessment is part of the target-setting process. Your school will have set up its own monitoring and assessment systems. Many schools are using QCA guidance on National Curriculum assessment.

> 'Ways of identifying the starting points for learning from which progress can be measured are an essential feature of any assessment system.' (QCA, 2001)

Examples include

- baseline assessment
- National Curriculum subject assessments.

The performance descriptions published in March 2001 have built on the P scales set out in 1998 in the DfEE/QCA booklet *Supporting the Target-Setting Process*. The P scales outline learning and attainment below Level 1 using eight descriptors from P1 to P8 and, in the 2001 document, they cover all National Curriculum subjects including citizenship, RE and PSHE. The levels P1 to P3 are common to all subjects but P4 to P8 show subject-specific attainment.

The descriptors can help with identifying starting points, setting targets, assessing attainment and charting progress. They include some subject-specific examples to support the identification of attainment at these early levels.

For you, as SEN coordinator, teacher assessment data and standardised test data act as useful signposts, but diagnostic data will give you the information needed to help you formulate an IEP.

Diagnostic data

For you as SEN coordinator, teacher assessment data and standardised test data act as useful signposts, but diagnostic data will give you the information needed to help you formulate an IEP. You need to collect resources for diagnostic assessment of specific areas of learning. If you have opportunities to meet with a specialist support teacher, ask his or her advice regarding the range and suitability of such tests.

Tests are available that will inform you about the way in which the child learns, by checking such things as

visual memory or short-term memory. You will be able to administer some of these tests yourself, while others should be carried out by trained personnel. More complex processes will need the experience and training only available to educational psychologists and other professionals.

Scores

All published assessment materials provide scores. The most common types of scores are outlined below.

Standardised score (SS)

This is an averaged score against a norm. The tests outlined in this chapter all provide standardised scores related to national averages. A rough guide to interpreting these results is as follows.

- A child who gains a standardised score of 100 is in the average range.
- A standardised score below 85 is a warning that the child may have special needs, which should be accommodated within a mainstream class setting.
- A score of below 70 would indicate a child needing significant help and probably a statement.

Raw score (RS)

This is the number of marks given for each answer before conversion into a standardised score, or a reading age score in some instances.

Use assessments to record both standardised scores and reading ages, as each provides useful information.

> ### Age at test date
>
> When calculating scores, have a list of the children's dates of birth with their ages in years and months. This age is counted from their date of birth until the test date. Whole months are counted to the test date. For example, if a child's date of birth was 11.11.91 and the test date was 16.4.02, count ten years to 11.11.01 then the five whole months to 11.4.02 = ten years, five months.

The table at the top of page 46 gives explanations of terminology found in assessment materials and psychologists' reports. The figures in the table have been rounded up and show the theoretical distribution of abilities for the population. This table is often represented as a curve sitting on a line, with extremes of ability at each end.

Distribution and meaning of test results				
Rounded percentage of population in each band	**Standardised scores (quotients)**	**Percentile ranks**	**Wechler associated qualitative descriptions**	**Associated educational needs/difficulties**
2%	55–70	0.1–2%	Exceptionally low	Significant to moderate learning difficulties. Specialist SEN provision likely.
14%	70–85	2–16%	Low to low average	Mild learning difficulties. Within-school help likely to be needed.
34%	85–100	16–50%	Low average to average (middle 50%)	Should cope with mainstream curriculum and ordinary teaching methods, unless significant emotional or behavioural difficulties.
34%	100–115	50–84%	Average to high average	Should cope well with mainstream curriculum and ordinary teaching methods unless significant emotional or behavioural difficulties.
14%	115–130	84–98%	High average to high	Should cope well with mainstream curriculum and ordinary teaching methods unless significant emotional or behavioural difficulties.
2%	130–145+	98–99.9%	Exceptionally high	Gifted or talented. Should undertake extension activities.

Working with your assessment coordinator

Effective management of SEN covers the whole school and curriculum, so it's important that you're on the senior management team and are able to work alongside the assessment coordinator. The assessment policy needs an SEN section and cross-references with the SEN policy. If there is a yearly assessment schedule, it should be referenced in the SEN policy. A schedule for a year group may look like the table below.

Assessment schedule should be in policy

Working closely with your assessment coordinator allows you to manage whole-school assessment issues effectively. It's common practice for SEN coordinators to keep the results of diagnostic and some formative tests, with all summative tests held centrally on a computer.

Where such a system is in use, you should be able to access and print results for children on the SEN register. The assessment coordinator should alert you to any child whose assessments cause concern.

Annual assessment schedule Year 2

Sept	Oct	Nov	Dec	Jan	Feb	March	April	May	June	July
Salford	High frequency words (HFWs)			Group Reading Test A or Suffolk Reading	HFWs	Salford	Maths 6 or 7 infer	SATs	HFWs	Reports

Selecting and using standardised tests

If the standardised test results are going to be used to make comparisons between groups of children or be used to track individual progress, schools need to purchase tests that are designed for use with the same children over a number of years such as the reading tests produced by nferNelson. Using different standardised tests from one year to another will not provide accurate comparisons.

What to look for when purchasing standardised tests

It is important to evaluate critically any standardised tests you may be considering, before purchasing them. Below is a series of questions that are worth considering before making your purchase.

1 **Is the test up to date?** Check the reliability and validity of the tests and the date of their standardisation. Also check that the language and vocabulary used are not outdated. Children will not be able to succeed in a test if its language is unfamiliar to them.

2 **Does the test meet the needs that it is being purchased for?** It is important for the test to meet your needs and some of the questions to consider are as follows.
   - Is it an appropriate test for your selected age range/s?
   - Does the test have an extension paper to meet the needs of the most able as well as an appropriate paper for children with special educational needs?
   - Can the test be given at your chosen point in the term or year?
   - Is the test designed for use over a number of years with the same children to enable the tracking of individual progress and comparison between groups of children?
   - Does the test assess your chosen reading skills, knowledge and attitudes? It is important to identify exactly what the test assesses. As a staff team, decide on the selection criteria. Do you want a test that assesses, for example, decoding skills, prediction, comprehension, personal response to texts, sight vocabulary, deduction and hypothesis or a combination of these?

3 **Does the test provide diagnostic information?** Bear in mind that certain tests can be more diagnostically useful than others. Look for one that indicates children's strengths and weaknesses, so that it can inform future planning, grouping and target-setting.

4 **Does the test complement your existing test materials and assessment activities?** It is likely that you will already have other testing materials available in school and will already carry out a range of assessment activities. The selected standardised test should complement these and should provide additional information and data to what is already available in school.

5 **Is the test easy to administer?** Schools are busy places and you will want to purchase a test that is easy to administer. Consider whether carrying out the test will require the support of extra adults, the use of additional furniture or the rearranging of classrooms. You may want to select a test that closely matches the way teachers usually work in their classrooms, or one that is similar in format to the end of key stage tests. Familiarity with the format and structure of the test will prove less stressful for children and teachers alike.

6 **Is the teacher's guidance or handbook user-friendly?** It is important to check that the teacher's guidance that comes with the test is easy to read and understand. A busy teacher will not want to spend valuable time ploughing through a difficult and poorly written handbook. The teacher's guidance should advise on whom the test is designed for, when it should be given, how to administer and mark it, how to produce the data and how to analyse it.

The initial outlay when purchasing a standardised test, together with buying further packs of the test papers, can be high, but if a school has critically evaluated the product before buying it, it should meet the needs of the school and provide value for money.

Additional information and advice on reading tests

The Curriculum Assessment Authority for Wales has produced a document entitled *Guidance on the Use of Standardised Reading Tests*. This informative guide reviews word recognition tests, tests used for screening purposes (using word/picture match or multiple-choice sentence completion) and standardised reading tests suitable for group or individual use.

It sets out to show the strengths and limitations of some of the most commonly used tests and it identifies their usefulness as part of a school's assessment package. The guide also indicates the most productive use of information derived from the tests.

Within the guide, there are examples of both school and LEA uses of standardised reading tests that can act as a model or as a discussion point when a school is considering its own use of these tests. A glossary briefly explains some of the most frequently used terms in standardised reading manuals. This is a useful section, both when purchasing a standardised reading test and when administering it.

A summary of several standardised tests is included in the guide, which can help you select the most appropriate test for the purposes you have in mind. The guide also outlines, in tabular form, the purpose and content of a variety of reading tests. It also provides additional information about when the tests were produced, the intended age range, how they are administered, the date of standardisation, scoring techniques and the reliability and validity of the tests.

Reading the guide could save you both time and money when you come to consider the acquisition of a standardised reading test.

Reporting your findings

If data from assessments is to have any practical use, and is to impact upon improving the standards in your school, you must devise systems for disseminating your findings to the right people. Key people in the school have a need and a right to know what is happening in terms of levels of achievement or patterns which have been identified in learning or behaviour. In carrying out assessments, you may reveal something which you must pass on to others who either need to know or are in a position to respond to your findings.

Reporting to the headteacher

The headteacher should be informed about all your findings on a termly basis. A duplicate copy of all your summative data should be presented, along with any conclusions you may have drawn. Discussion with the head may shed more light on some of the issues and, with his or her wider knowledge of the school, may indicate areas for further research, or involve changes in teaching methods. It may be something for you to undertake from a special needs angle, or it may more likely become a whole-school issue.

If there is some serious concern arising from the data you have shown to the head, they may need to see the raw data, so make sure this is available and in a form that can be easily read by a third party.

Reporting to the governors

The governors, especially the SEN governor, should also receive termly summative data on any issue that forms part of the school improvement plan. You should also provide a written conclusion regarding progress towards targets and any patterns which are emerging and which may need to be incorporated into the long-term plan.

When writing their annual report to parents, the governors will need data to show the make up of the special needs register. This should include data benchmarked against the school's own data from the previous year, as well as across other schools of this type. Governors will also need a summary of the range of conditions and needs catered for and any trends that may have appeared, together with the context if known (such as a rise in the prevalence of this condition across all schools in your authority).

Reporting to your colleagues

Your colleagues will be providing you with some of your assessment data. If this is feeding into a wider picture then they should know about it as soon as possible. For example, if you collected data about spelling standards because of low grades in the end of key stage tests, the teachers will need to see the range of this problem. What is happening and why? Is it starting at a particular age or stage? Is it a particular group of children? Are boys' standards markedly worse or better than girls'? Data can provide the answers to these and other similar questions. Staff awareness, discussion and training can start to change the situation.

Data about an individual child needs to be fed back very quickly to the class teacher and, where appropriate, to the teaching assistant who may be working with the child. Unless this data is shared, the child's progress will be delayed. Arrange time to talk to the teacher when you can be free from interruption and make sure that you allow enough time to deal with all the issues that could arise. You will need to

1 allow enough time to go through all the facts shown by the data (on achievements, learning processes and/or behaviour)

2 discuss possible reasons for the problems

3 discuss ways forward, taking into account
- levels of support and methods of intervention
- jointly drawing up an IEP (involving the parents and the child)
- how the work will be monitored and evaluated
- a timescale for doing all of this.

Reporting to parents

Parents need to know about their own child. Following on from the discussion with the child's class teacher, you will need to talk to the parents. They will be able to take part, to a certain extent, in drawing up their child's IEP. To set the child's targets you will need to refer to the data you have collected. When reporting to parents, bear in mind the following points.

- Always consider the needs of the parents and the way in which a partnership with the parents will enhance the effectiveness of your work with the child.

- Remember that the majority of parents will need explanations given in everyday language, not educational jargon.

- Have examples of the actual work the child did, not just the raw data.

- Explain what the child should be able to do and where the child needs help to achieve these levels.

- Be positive but truthful.

- Have some ideas ready for things the parents might do to help the child at home.

Using data

Nothing will fundamentally change in your school or for your children unless you apply this information to setting targets for improvement. Setting targets completes one cycle of assessment and begins the next.

Diagnostic tests will provide you with a clear guide as to the next step the child needs to take and the next milestone they need to reach. This will feed into the next assessment you make, ensuring that you can measure progress effectively.

When making referrals for statutory assessment, you will need to submit both raw data and referenced data. You will also need the actual test papers to substantiate your findings and your interpretations. Comparative results from earlier assessments will demonstrate any lack of progress made by the child despite your interventions.

Test materials

A range of test materials available for assessing children's reading, cognitive and maths abilities is reviewed below. All are designed to be used across a range of ages.

The nferNelson website has information about all their assessments. Of particular interest is the Test Enabler series for users of SIMS assessment manager. This can be used in conjunction with certain nferNelson tests, where tests can be marked on the computer. It automatically calculates scores, provides individual and group profiles, and stores test results for the whole school.

Reading tests

British Picture Vocabulary Scale (BPVS11) (nferNelson)

Age range 3–15 years.

Scoring Standardised score.

Time needed 5–8 minutes.

Purpose Assesses language impairment, low/high ability.

Comments An individual diagnostic test. Picture cards are used throughout, so it is very useful as a means of showing progress for children of any age who cannot read.

Individual Reading Analysis (IRA – originally MIRA) (nferNelson)

Age range 5 years 6 months–11 years 2 months.

Scoring Standardised score, reading age.

Time needed 5–15 minutes.

Purpose Tests reading accuracy and comprehension.

Comments An individual diagnostic test. Children need to know about 70 high frequency words to score above base 1 (SS 60+).

Suffolk Reading Scale (nferNelson)

Age range In three levels: 6–7 years, 8–10 years, 11 years–14 years 11 months.

Scoring Standardised score, reading age.

Time needed 20 minutes, whole class, with parallel forms.

Purpose Assesses reading ability.

Comments A summative test used by many LEAs as an area test. Not for non-readers at it is multiple choice, which means they can guess, circling in a pattern, and get a false score showing average ability.

Salford Sentence Reading Test (Hodder Headline)

Age range 5–9 years.

Scoring Standardised score, reading age.

Time needed 2–3 minutes on an individual basis.

Purpose Assesses children who are not making progress in reading.

Comments A summative test. The test has been revised and brought up to date using new norms. The revised test has two equivalent forms (X and Y). each form has 13 sentences with the sentences becoming gradually more difficult.

The laminated test cards X and Y can be reused and the record sheet can be used not only for scoring but also for analysis. This is a simple, quick test to administer and it can be used with the same children each year by alternating the test cards.

Primary Reading Test (nferNelson)

Age range In two levels: 5 years 9 months–10 years 2 months and 6 years 9 months–12 years 2 months.

Scoring Standardised score, reading age.

Time needed 20–30 minutes; parallel forms for whole class.

Purpose Tests reading and understanding.

Comments A summative test. Multiple choice, including pictures at beginning of Level 1. There is considerable discrepancy between scores for this and for IRA and Salford.

The Parallel Spelling Tests (Hodder Headline)

Age range Provides spelling quotients from 6 years 6 months–13 years and spelling ages from 6 years–15 years.

Scoring Standardised score. spelling quotients and spelling ages.

Time needed 20 minutes.

Purpose Enables spelling progress to be charted from Year 2 to Year 7.

Comments A word is spoken, then put into a sentence (provided in the test) and given again. Several choices are provided to avoid children remembering from one test to the next. You can use the results to build on strengths and identify weaknesses.

Cognitive ability tests

Cognitive Profiling System (CoPs 1) (Lucid Research)

Age range 4 years–8 years 11 months.

Scoring This is computer generated as a graphical profile of each child's cognitive abilities using standardised norms.

Time needed Flexible according to the needs of each child.

Purpose This is a computerised psychometric assessment system. It uses a set of eight games to provide direct assessment of different aspects of cognitive ability. These are

- visual/spatial sequential memory (spatial/temporal)
- visual/verbal sequential memory (symbolic)
- auditory/visual associative memory
- auditory/verbal sequential memory
- visual/verbal associative learning
- phonological awareness
- auditory discrimination
- colour discrimination.

Comments *CoPs 1* provides information about strengths and weaknesses and therefore assists you in planning differentiated activities to meet children's needs. You might want to consider using *Quick CoPs*, which reduces the number of games from eight to four.

Maths tests

GOAL Formative Assessment in Key Stage 2 Mathematics (Hodder Headline)

Age range 7–11 years.

Scoring The test gives a National Curriculum level (A–C) as well as a standardised score. It also provides an analysis of skills (knowledge and understanding, problem solving and calculation) based on Bloom's taxonomy of higher-order thinking skills.

Time needed 45 minutes to administer to a class.

Purpose This formative test has been designed to support teachers in monitoring both individual and class progress. It is matched to National Curriculum levels and the National Numeracy Strategy programmes of study. It helps teachers to

- measure children's progress over time
- diagnose individual areas of strength and weakness
- compare standards of attainment year on year.

Comments A child-friendly test that provides a clear skills analysis. This helps teachers to develop more effective teaching strategies in order to support children's learning. The GOAL Formative Assessment tests can be used with mixed-ability groups.

Mathematics 6–14 (nferNelson)

Age range Nine levels from 6 years–15 years 2 months.

Scoring Standardised score.

Time needed Untimed but for whole class administered orally.

Purpose Tests skills and understanding of maths.

Comments A summative/diagnostic test. You can profile the strengths and weaknesses of individuals, classes and the whole school. Results are quite accurate for predicting grades. The nferNelson website has a table which gives equivalent levels and grades at GCSE.

Group Mathematics Test (Hodder Headline)

Age range 6 years 4 months–11 years 10 months.

Scoring Standardised score.

Time needed 20 minutes, parallel papers for whole class, partly administered orally, then addition and subtraction computation sections.

Purpose General assessment.

Comments This test focuses on numerical computation and includes some orally-presented questions. This enables teachers to identify those children whose reading difficulties may be masking their maths ability.

Addresses

Desktop Publications
54 Railway Street
Barnetby-le-Wold
North Lincolnshire DN38 6DQ
Tel: 01652 688781
www.desktoppublications.co.uk

Hodder Headline
338 Euston Road
London NW1 3BH
Tel: 020 7873 6000_
www.hodderheadline.co.uk

Lucid Research Ltd
PO Box 63
Beverley
East Yorkshire HU17 8ZZ
Tel: 01482 466158
www.lucid-research.com

nferNelson
Darville House
2 Oxford Road East
Windsor
Berkshire SL4 1DF
www.nfer-nelson.co.uk

QCA Publications
PO Box 99
Sudbury
Suffolk CO10 2SN
Tel: 01787 884 444
www.qcashop.org.uk

SIMS
Capita Education Services Ltd
Stannard Way
Priory Business Park
Cardington
Bedford MK44 3SG
Tel: 01234 838080
www.sims.co.uk

The document *Guidance on the Use of Standardised Reading Tests* is available from
ACCAC Publications
7th Floor
Southgate House
Wood Street
Cardiff CF10 1EW
Tel: 02920 375 400
Email: info@accac.org.uk

References

DfEE (1998) *Supporting the Target-Setting Process.* Ref. STSS. London: DfEE.

QCA (2001) *Planning, Teaching and Assessing the Curriculum for Pupils with Learning Difficulties.* Ref. QCA/01/736. London: QCA.

Thanks to Jane Calver, Lynn Cousins, Diane Davies, Anne Philips and Christabel Reynish for their contributions to this chapter.

CHAPTER 4
Strategies for learning

This chapter looks at some of the skills needed for learning and identifies the most common problems encountered by children who have difficulty in developing these skills. It is important to remember that many children who encounter difficulties in one area may have strengths in another and may find learning easier if their strengths are utilised. The activities suggested to develop specific skills are not intended to be exhaustive, but rather to act as a starting point.

Applying strategies

The suggested activities should not be considered in isolation, as just a list of skills to be mastered, but rather as activities that can often be incorporated into a class-based lesson for the benefit of all children, and especially for those children who are identified as having special needs. Many of the activities can be adapted to link with different areas of the curriculum and are designed to enhance the learning process.

> 'Differentiation of learning activities within the primary curriculum framework will help schools to meet the learning needs of all children ... Schools should not assume that children's learning difficulties always result solely, or even mainly, from problems within the child. A school's own practices make a difference – for good or ill.' (DfES, 2001 – 6:18)

All children should be given as many opportunities as possible to transfer and generalise the skills they learn in order to ensure that the skills remain in their long-term memory. Some of the activities suggested can be differentiated within the whole-class situation. Other activities may be more suitable for group sessions and these could be incorporated into literacy and numeracy hours, or other areas of the curriculum. For example, differentiated auditory discrimination activities could be part of music or science lessons.

Games and group activities

Taking part in games and group activities allows children to develop a shared understanding of language as they talk and listen to each other. It provides them with a context for their learning and is particularly important for those children with special needs. Some children will come from language-rich homes and will be confident speakers and listeners. Other children may come from backgrounds where they have been given little opportunity to use language in a variety of situations. These children may have poor self-esteem and may be unwilling to take an active part in group sessions initially. They may need to start with paired activities. This can then be extended by two pairs being asked to share their games and activities with each other.

Games and group activities give teachers and other adults the opportunity to observe, assess and monitor children's progress. In this way the children's strengths can be recognised and their preferred learning styles incorporated into the different activities.

How this chapter works

We start by looking at the importance of visual, auditory and kinaesthetic (VAK) learning styles as gateways to children's learning. Subsequent pages provide descriptions of specific learning skills (terms that are often given in professionals' assessment reports of SEN children) and concepts, together with a range of activities which can be used to strengthen these skills and a list of publishers of appropriate materials.

At the end of this chapter you will find a useful summary record sheet which identifies those skills and concepts which need to be addressed for each individual SEN child in each class or year-group.

Reference
DfES (2001) *Special Educational Needs Code of Practice.*
Ref: 581/2001. London: DfES.

VAK learning styles

Visual, auditory and kinaesthetic (VAK) are terms for ways in which we give and receive information. These are often referred to as teaching and learning styles. If an individual tends to present information through pictures, charts, audio-visual aids and diagrams then they have a visual teaching style. Similarly, a child who learns best in this way has a predominantly visual learning style. Most children have a 'preferred learning style' or a way of learning that suits them best. Some children have a 'dominant learning style' and have difficulty accessing information unless they are able to use this style. If children are given opportunities to learn using their strengths then they are more successful. They tend to learn in a more natural way, making learning easier and more enjoyable.

As teachers we need to be aware that we should vary our teaching style in order to accommodate the learning needs of all our children. Sometimes we need to present information using a balance of teaching styles, in order to allow learners to experience not only their own preferred learning styles but to be able to collaborate with other learners who have different learning styles.

These are some of the most common characteristics of children with different learning styles.

Visual

Visual learners enjoy learning through written language and visual materials. They often have visual/spatial strengths. They like to

- use diagrams, graphs and charts
- relate text to illustrations
- design posters to convey information
- use mind-maps
- use cue cards and prompt sheets
- refer to wall charts and visual organisers
- use visual memory spelling techniques
- use visualisation techniques for story writing
- enjoy working on computer graphics
- use videos and films to gain information.

Auditory

Auditory learners like to learn through listening. They also enjoy talking about their learning. They like to

- take part in guided group reading activities
- share their ideas in circletime
- play language and word games
- take part in role play
- take an active part in collaborative group work
- talk about their written work
- join in saying aloud rhymes, chants and performance poetry
- take part in auditory discrimination games and activities
- listen to audio tapes or CDs
- take part in musical activities.

Kinaesthetic

Kinaesthetic learners like to learn through movement and touch. They often find it difficult to keep still. They like to

- have regular 'brain breaks' interspersed between learning sessions
- use whiteboards and highlighter pens
- use magnetic numbers and letters for support with literacy and numeracy
- take part in IT control activities
- learn through using their senses
- take an active part in movement and mime
- play language and word games
- learn through practical/concrete activities
- use constructional apparatus
- use a range of media in art.

If we try to provide an effective learning environment for children with learning difficulties then we will enhance the learning of all our children. It is important to ensure that this environment encourages all the children to be open to each other's learning needs. If we show that we value children's individual strengths then they will learn to value each other and enjoy sharing the experience of learning.

Auditory discrimination

Auditory discrimination is the ability to detect similarities and differences when listening to sounds. This could involve being able to discriminate between larger sounds made by animals, vehicles, etc., or it could involve being able to detect similarities and differences between sounds in words.

Children who have difficulties in this area may have

- problems identifying speech sounds
- poor listening skills, especially when there is background noise
- difficulty discriminating between similar words
- difficulty with rhyming activities
- poor articulation of sounds and words
- kinaesthetic strengths (and learn better through using concrete materials and practical experiences)
- visual strengths (and enjoy learning through using visual materials such as charts, maps, videos, demonstrations)
- good motor skills (and have strengths in design and technology, art, PE and games).

Activities to develop auditory discrimination skills

1 **Listening 1** – listen to sounds on tape – there are a number of materials available or you can make your own – then ask the children to
   - point to a picture of the object making the sound and name it
   - point to a real object that makes the sound and then try it out.
2 **Listening 2** – listen to the sound of real objects with eyes closed. Children guess and name.
3 **Sound bingo** – listening to sounds on tape and covering the correct picture.
4 **Sound walk** – children drawing pictures or writing down the names of the sounds they hear on the walk.
5 **Grouping sounds** – animals, musical instruments, vehicles, etc.
6 **Odd one out** – ask the children to identify the sound that is not part of a group of sounds, eg. dog barking, pig grunting, cow mooing, musical instrument playing.
7 **Musical discrimination** – discriminating between loud/quiet, high/low, fast/slow notes. This should be part of a music lesson – ask a TA to observe.

8 **Clapping or tapping rhythms** – you can use children's names and polysyllable words. This activity can be linked with picture-noun recognition. Children can work in pairs, using picture-noun cards – take turns to clap syllable beats and choose the picture-noun card to match the number of beats.
9 **Same/different 1** – ask the children to listen to sets of two everyday sounds and identify those that are the same and those that are different.
10 **Same/different 2** – ask the children to listen to sets of two words and identify those that are the same and those that are different, eg. bat/bat, bat/bet.
11 **Same/different 3** – ask the children to listen to sets of two words and identify those that rhyme and those that don't, eg. cat/mat, bed/bud.
12 **Hands up 1** – ask the children to put up their hands when they hear a particular sound (sounds given one at a time).
13 **Hands up 2** – ask the children to put up their hands when they hear a particular sound against a background of other sounds (figure/ground auditory discrimination).
14 **Who is it?** – choose a child to be blindfolded, then ask another child to say a short sentence. Ask the blindfolded child to identify the other child by name.
15 **Sound bingo** – discriminating between initial sounds.
16 **Rhyme time** – ask the children to listen to a word. If it rhymes with the word that they have in their hand then they can keep it. The winner is the first person who collects five rhyming words.

Publishers and suppliers

The following publishers and suppliers have a number of support materials to help children develop auditory discrimination skills.

- Galt
- Hope Education
- LDA
- Philip and Tacey
- R-E-M
- Select Educational Equipment
- Wesco
- Winslow

(See pages 69–70 for details.)

Phonological awareness

Phonological awareness is the ability to be aware of sounds within words and to be able to break down words into syllables and into phonemes. Research shows that awareness of larger units of sound like syllables and onset and rime develop earlier than phonemic awareness.

Children who have difficulties in this area may have

- problems identifying syllables in polysyllabic words
- problems recognising rhyming words
- difficulty in generating rhyme
- difficulty identifying initial, medial and final phonemes in words
- difficulty with phoneme blending
- visual strengths (learning better from charts, diagrams, videos, demonstrations and other visual materials)
- a good visual memory (being able to visualise information and present it in the form of mind-maps, diagrams, charts, posters, illustrations)
- kinaesthetic strengths (learning better through using concrete materials, practical experiences and multisensory techniques).

Activities to develop phonological awareness skills

1 **Syllable coun**t – say the word (eg. yesterday), then use fingers to count the syllables (yes/ter/day).

2 **Finish the name** – adult to say the first syllable of a two syllable name (eg. Hen...), then ask the child to complete it (Henry).

3 **Finish the word** – adult to say the first syllable of a two syllable word (eg. zeb...), then ask the child to complete it (zebra).

4 **I spy 1** – initial sounds (everyday items in the classroom).

5 **I spy 2** – initial sounds (pictorial choice).

6 **Pairs** – matching pictures to initial sounds.

7 **Bingo** – matching pictures to initial sounds.

8 **I spy 3** – 'I went to the zoo/park/seaside and saw something beginning with...' (initial sounds).

9 **Sound/picture mapping** – match picture to sound by drawing lines.

10 **I spy 4** – initial CV blending (I am thinking of something beginning with ca...).

11 **Pelmanism** – matching pictures to initial CV.

12 **Missing vowels** – helps the children to become aware that there could be more than one choice of vowels for each word (eg. b_t – bat, bet, bit, but).

13 **Line-links** – ask the children to draw lines to link initial sounds to rhyme endings (eg. b–ed/r–ed, m–an/c–an).

14 **Rhyme wordsearches**.

15 **Rhyme pelmanism 1** – pictorial.

16 **Rhyme pelmanism 2** – words.

17 **Rhyme families 1** – collect rhyming pictures ('Can I have a picture that rhymes with ...').

18 **Rhyme families 2** – collect rhyming words ('Can I have a word that rhymes with...').

19 **Rhyming cloze (oral)** – using traditional rhymes, action rhymes, songs and jingles.

20 **Blends and ends** – matching initial consonant blends to rhyme endings (eg. bl—ack/tr—ack).

21 **Dominoes** – using blends and ends.

22 **Tongue twisters** – initial sounds and consonant blends (eg. six silly swans swam out to sea).

23 **Odd word out** – both oral and written (eg. ring, sing, song, thing).

24 **Sense or nonsense** – ask the children to identify the words that make sense by blending the phonemes (eg. brick, quick, stick, smick, trick).

25 **Compound word pairs** – collect word pairs (eg. sea/side, tea/pot)

26 **Syllable sort** – collect syllables to form polysyllabic words (eg. yes/ter/day, af/ter/noon)

Publishers and suppliers

The following publishers and suppliers have a number of support materials to help children develop phonological awareness skills.

- AVP
- Crossbow Educational
- Easylearn
- Egon Publishers Ltd
- Formative Fun
- Galt
- HELP Educational Games
- Hope Education
- Hopscotch Educational Publishing Ltd
- Hilda King Educational
- Learning Materials
- LDA
- Philip and Tacey
- Psychological Corp (Harcourt) – for the Phonological Abilities Test (PAT)
- Select Educational
- Thrass (UK) Ltd
- Whurr Publishers

(See pages 69–70 for details.)

Visual discrimination

Visual discrimination is the ability to recognise similarities and differences between visual images. These images could be pictures, objects, words or letters.

Children who have difficulties in this area may

- be unable to identify shades of colour and texture in pictures
- confuse shapes and symbols in maths
- confuse letters, words and objects that look similar
- reverse numbers and letters when writing
- have problems with learning sight vocabulary
- find simple scanning activities difficult (eg. wordsearches, dictionary work, using an index)
- have problems with comparative language (eg. taller than, shorter than, longer than)
- have difficulty completing jigsaw puzzles
- have problems with copying from the board
- prefer to use multisensory strategies when learning
- work with small amounts of visual material at a time
- use audio tapes for gathering and conveying information
- predominantly use phonic strategies when reading.

Activities to develop visual discrimination skills

1 **Sorting** – for colour, shape, size and texture.
2 **Post-a-shape** – matching shapes to the correct opening.
3 **Matching silhouettes 1** – pictorial.
4 **Matching silhouettes 2** – shapes.
5 **Pairs 1** – matching objects, shapes, pictures.
6 **Odd one out 1** – colour, shape, size.
7 **Odd one out 2** – pictorial (apple, orange, banana, cup).
8 **Pairs 1** – matching letters, using a choice of only four to six at first. Try to avoid the letters that are easily confused like b, d and p. Introduce those letters gradually.
9 **Pairs 2** – matching numerals, using a choice of only four or five at first.
10 **Matching sequences** – colour, shape and size.
11 **Spot the difference** – searching for visual similarities and differences between two pictures.

12 **Mix and match** – making three-part flip-books, where heads, bodies and tails of animals can be interchanged.
13 **Match the detail** – matching a picture of a detail (such as a window) to the picture from which the detail comes (such as the house that has that window).
14 **Shapewords** – matching high frequency words to a shape outline.
15 **Snap** – matching a range of pictorial cards.
16 **Lotto** – matching word to word.
17 **Dominoes** – matching picture to picture or word to word.
18 **Words to sentence matching**.
19 **Spot the difference** – searching for visual similarities and differences in words.
20 **Letter change** (eg. cat, cot, cut)
21 **Onset change** (eg. sent, tent, went).
22 **Odd word out** – both oral and written (eg. hand, land, lend, stand).
23 **Pelmanism 1** – rhyming picture pairs.
24 **Pelmanism 2** – rhyming word pairs.
25 **Wordsearches** – using high frequency words or rhyming words.

Publishers and suppliers
The following publishers and suppliers have a number of support materials to help children develop visual discrimination skills.

- AVP
- Formative Fun
- Galt
- Hope Education
- LDA
- Philip and Tacey
- R-E-M
- Rompa
- Select Educational Equipment
- Taskmaster
- Wesco
- Winslow

(See pages 69–70 for details.)

Visual memory

Visual memory is the ability to recall information that has been presented visually. The information may be retained for a short while (short-term memory), rehearsed and retained for a longer period of time (long-term memory), or retained and recalled in the correct sequence (visual sequential memory).

Children who have difficulties in this area may

- have immature drawing skills (drawings lack detail)
- have problems with learning sight vocabulary
- have difficulty with letter and number orientation
- find reading music difficult
- be unable to recall patterns, shapes and designs
- have spelling difficulties
- enjoy using multisensory strategies when learning
- use audio tapes to aid recall of information
- have strengths in logic, verbal and non-verbal reasoning skills
- have kinaesthetic strengths (learn better when actively involved in a lesson through movement and touch).

Activities to develop visual memory skills

1 **Recall object features** – let the children look at an object and talk about its features. Then take the object away and ask them to recall some of its features.

2 **Recall picture details** – let the children look at a picture and talk about the details. Then take the picture away and ask them to recall some of the details.

3 **Complete the shape** – show the children a shape and then give them an incomplete drawing of the same shape. Ask the children to complete the shape from memory.

4 **Complete the picture** – show the children a simple picture and then give them an incomplete drawing of the same picture. Ask the children to complete the picture from memory.

5 **What's missing?** – show the children two similar pictures and ask them to identify what is missing from one of the pictures.

6 **Kim's game** – place some everyday objects on a table. Show them to the children for about a minute, then cover them and see how many each can recall. This can also be played by taking one object away and asking the children to identify the object that is missing.

7 **Pelmanism** – shapes, objects, animals, etc.

8 **Cause and effect** – pictorial visual memory sequence.

9 **Recall and sequence 1** – a series of three to four coloured shapes.

10 **Recall and sequence 2** – a series of three to four pictures (eg. everyday situations, life sequences).

11 **Recall and sequence 3** – a series of three to four pictures (telling a story).

12 **What happens next?** – complete pictorial action sequences related to everyday situations.

13 **Recall and sequence 4** – a series of three to four words in a sentence.

14 **Recall and sequence 5** – the alphabet, using magnetic letters.

15 **Recall and sequence 6** – the days of the week using magnetic words.

16 **Recall and sequence 7** – magnetic numbers.

17 **Word bingo** – simple high frequency words.

18 **Visual memory spelling games** – using the look, cover, remember, write, check strategy with simple high frequency words.

Publishers and suppliers

The following publishers and suppliers have a number of support materials to help children develop visual memory skills.

- AVP
- Formative Fun
- Galt
- Hope Education
- LDA
- Philip and Tacey
- R-E-M
- Rompa
- Select Educational Equipment
- Taskmaster
- Wesco
- Winslow

(See pages 69–70 for details.)

Verbal comprehension

Verbal comprehension is the ability to listen to information that has been given orally, then remember it, understand it and use the information across a range of tasks.

Children who have difficulty in this area may

- have problems with understanding oral directions and instructions
- be easily distracted by classroom noise
- have poor attention and listening skills
- often ask for repetition of what has been said
- have some word-finding difficulties
- have reading comprehension problems
- have difficulty following more complex discussions
- have difficulty understanding information without visual and concrete cues
- give inappropriate answers to questions
- have difficulty in understanding abstract concepts
- have poor organisational skills
- have kinaesthetic strengths (learning better when actively involved in a lesson through movement and touch)
- have visual/spatial strengths (learn better from charts, diagrams, videos, demonstrations and other visual materials)
- have good motor skills (and have strengths in design and technology, art, PE and games).

Activities to develop verbal comprehension skills

1 **Following directions 1** – in the classroom (eg. 'Come and sit on the carpet', 'Line up by the door').

2 **Simon says** – using body movements (eg. 'Stand on one leg', 'Raise one arm').

3 **Following directions 2** – during PE, games and other physical activities.

4 **Following instructions 1** – using possessives (eg. 'Put the book on *my* table').

5 **Following instructions 2** – using adjectives (eg. 'Pick up the *red* ball').

6 **Following instructions 3** – using the language of time (eg. 'You can go out to play *after* you have put the toys away').

7 **Listen and colour** – eg. 'Colour the big fish red and the little fish green.'

8 **Yes or no** – true or false statements (eg. 'A pig can fly. A fish can swim.')

9 **Sense or nonsense 1** – ask children to listen and identify the sentence that makes sense.

10 **Match sentences to the correct pictures 1** – using high frequency verbs (eg. 'The girl *is jumping*').

11 **Match sentences to the correct pictures 2** – using prepositions (eg. 'The cat is *in* the box').

12 **Match sentences to the correct picture 3** – using high frequency nouns (eg. '*Mum* is in the *garden*').

13 **Sense or nonsense 2** – read, write and draw only those sentences that make sense.

14 **What am I?** – Listen and identify the item from a specific category (eg. animal, fruit, object) from oral sentence clues.

15 **What next?** – oral story prediction.

16 **Everyday questions** – adult to model asking questions related to familiar events and experiences (eg. 'What did you do at the seaside?' 'Who went to the seaside with you?'). Children then ask questions of each other related to familiar events and experiences.

17 **Following instructions 4** – follow a simple instruction sequence for a classroom activity using both pictorial and written clues.

18 **Time sequence** – draw a flow chart of the main events in a story.

19 **Who am I?** – ask the children to guess the person after listening to sentence clues (eg. story characters, occupations).

20 **Where am I?** – ask the children to choose a location on a picture map after listening to sentence clues (using prepositions, left and right).

21 **Cause and effect** – ask the children to complete a sentence orally (eg. 'The tree fell down because....,' 'The cat ran up into the tree because...').

22 **Why? Because** – story character motivation activities.

Publishers and suppliers

The following publishers and suppliers have a number of support materials to help children develop verbal comprehension skills.

- AVP
- Easylearn
- Formative Fun
- Galt
- Hope Education
- Learning Materials
- LDA

- Philip and Tacey
- R-E-M
- Wesco
- Winslow

(See pages 69–70 for details.)

Visual perception

Visual perception is the ability to recognise, interpret and organise visual images.

Children who have difficulties in this area may

- have a poor sense of direction
- have difficulties with organisational skills
- reverse words in both reading and spelling (eg. saw for was)
- have difficulty understanding abstract maths concepts, particularly in the areas of shape, space and measure
- have problems with comparative language (eg. taller than, shorter than, longer than)
- have difficulty completing jigsaw puzzles
- have problems with copying from the board
- have problems with interpreting and organising diagrams, charts, graphs, maps and other visual methods of recording
- have difficulties judging speed and distance
- have difficulty with letter and number orientation
- have difficulty with structuring and organising written work
- have strengths in logic, verbal and non-verbal reasoning skills
- enjoy using multisensory strategies when learning
- use audio tapes to aid recall of information
- prefer a phonic approach to learning to read
- prefer to use audio methods of recording information.

Activities to develop visual perception skills

1 **Post-a-shape** – matching shapes to the correct opening.

2 **Feely bag** – ask the children to describe a shape or object by feeling it without looking, then describe it again when they can see it.

3 **Copying 1** – a shape pattern or picture, using a magnetic board and pieces.

4 **What's missing? 1** – complete a 2D shape.

5 **What's missing? 2** – complete a picture.

6 **Guess what?** – ask the children to guess the object when only part is visible. A picture of an object could be cut into four pieces and only one part given at a time until the children have guessed what it is.

7 **Object/picture matching** – using everyday objects.

8 **Jigsaw puzzles** – of varying degrees of difficulty to suit individual children.

9 **Matching shape to silhouette** – using the correct orientation.

10 **Matching picture to silhouette** – using the correct orientation.

11 **Draw a person** – ask children to copy the features of a real person, then compare.

12 **Copying 2** – 2D shape patterns and pictures of varying degrees of difficulty.

13 **Colouring 1** – symmetrical patterns of varying degrees of difficulty to suit individual children.

14 **Colouring 2** – symmetrical pictures of varying degrees of difficulty to suit individual children.

15 **Tessellation 1** – arranging magnetic 2D shapes on a board.

16 **Tessellation 2** – drawing around 2D shapes.

17 **Sensory maze activities** – using a variety of materials.

18 **PE activities** – involving directional and positional language. Use symbols as a reminder.

19 **Multi-link pattern cards** – and similar activities.

20 **Instructions** – follow auditory instructions while using a diagram or picture, to show how to build a model.

21 **Noughts and crosses** – using plastic or wooden pieces.

22 **Computer-aided picture and design activities**.

23 **Brain gym** – some activities help to develop perceptual skills.

Publishers and suppliers

The following publishers and suppliers have a number of support materials to help children develop visual perception skills.

- AVP
- Edu-K – produces books about brain gym
- Formative Fun
- David Fulton publish *Developmental Dyspraxia* by Madeline Portwood
- Galt
- Hope Education
- LDA
- Philip and Tacey
- Rompa
- Select Educational Equipment
- Wesco
- Winslow

(See pages 69–70 for details.)

Auditory memory

Auditory memory is the ability to recall information that has been given orally. The information may be retained for a short while (short-term memory), rehearsed and retained for a longer period of time (long-term memory) or retained and recalled in the correct sequence (auditory sequential memory).

Children who have difficulties in this area may

- be unable to retain more than one or two items of information from a lesson presented orally

- have difficulty recalling information after a period of time, unless given specific support strategies

- have difficulty recalling information in the correct sequence

- have visual/spatial strengths (learn better from charts, diagrams, videos, demonstrations and other visual materials)

- have a good visual memory (be able to visualise information and present it in the form of mind-maps, diagrams, charts, posters, illustrations)

- have kinaesthetic strengths (learn better when actively involved in a lesson through movement and touch).

Activities to develop auditory memory skills

1 **Repeat and use information** – children could be asked to repeat a sequence of two or three colours and then thread beads or arrange cubes using that sequence. The children could also complete card number sequences in the same way.

2 **Reciting** – action rhymes, songs and jingles. Use the actions to aid the recall of key learning points.

3 **Memory and sequencing songs** – songs like 'Old Macdonald', 'Ten Green Bottles', 'One Man went to Mow'.

4 **Story recall 1** – retell the main events of a story, using puppets and background scenery as cues.

5 **Story recall 2** – draw the main events in well-known, patterned stories (eg. 'Little Red Hen', 'The Gingerbread Man').

6 **My grandmother went to market** – using real shopping items or pictures. Children have to recall the sequence of items bought.

7 **Recall simple sequences** – of personal experiences and events and share with the group or class.

8 **Recall verbal messages 1** – containing one or two elements and requiring a yes or no reply.

9 **Recall verbal messages 2** – containing one or two elements and requiring a simple sentence reply.

10 **Instructions** – recall and repeat task instructions containing one, then two, then three elements.

11 **Drawing 1** – story sequences from memory.

12 **Drawing 2** – the sequence of a simple activity.

13 **Explain** – the sequence of a simple activity.

14 **Recall** – days and events of the week.

15 **Alphabet sequences** – dot to dot, games and puzzles.

16 **Alphabet name game** – recall the sequence of the alphabet using children's names.

17 **Alphabet word game** – Recall the sequence of the alphabet when using simple word banks.

18 **Draw a time sequence** – flow chart of the main events in a story.

19 **Organise sentences** – in the correct sequence, relating to a school event, using words and phrases that signal time as cues (eg. after that, next).

20 **Mind-maps** – show the children how to use mind-maps to aid recall of key information.

Publishers and suppliers

The following publishers and suppliers have a number of support materials to help children develop auditory memory skills.

- AVP
- Buzan Centres (mind-mapping techniques)
- Formative Fun
- Galt
- Hope Education
- LDA
- Philip and Tacey
- R-E-M
- Wesco
- Winslow

(See pages 69–70 for details.)

Spatial awareness

Spatial awareness is the ability to be aware of oneself in space. Awareness of spatial relationships is the ability to see two or more objects in relation to each other and to oneself.

Children who have difficulties in this area may

- have poor presentation skills (can be unsure of how to arrange information on a page)
- have difficulty with structuring and organising written work
- have some visual perception difficulties
- appear clumsy and bump into objects when moving around the classroom
- have problems with positional language and be unable to tell left from right
- have difficulty playing games or doing PE, using apparatus
- have difficulty understanding abstract maths concepts, particularly in the areas of shape and space
- have problems with reproducing patterns and shapes
- have good auditory memory skills
- be confident speakers and listeners
- have good verbal comprehension skills
- have strengths in verbal and non-verbal reasoning
- enjoy using multisensory strategies when learning.

Activities to develop spatial awareness skills

1 **Action songs** – using different parts of the body.

2 **Movement games** – requiring the children to use space and position.

3 **Following directions** – during PE, games and other physical activities.

4 **Line-walking** – ask the children to walk along a line of chalk on the floor. Then ask them to walk along the left side of the line, then the right side of the line.

5 **Follow the leader** – put the children into groups of about eight. Then appoint one child as the leader. The others have to follow the leader and copy their actions as they go. Change the leader after a couple of minutes.

6 **Climbing activities** – using a range of large and small apparatus.

7 **Balancing activities** – using a range of both small and large apparatus.

8 **Jigsaw puzzles** – of varying degrees of difficulty to suit individual children.

9 **Brain gym** – some activities help to develop spatial awareness skills.

10 **Draw a person** – encourage children to look carefully at the position of the features on a real person.

11 **Patterns 1** – use dots as guidelines to reproduce a pattern.

12 **Patterns 2** – multi-link pattern cards and other activities.

13 **Footsteps** – ask the children to arrange cardboard footprints for others in the group to follow. Ensure that each footprint is marked with either 'left' or 'right.'

14 **Twister** – a proprietory game in which children have to ensure that different parts of their body are touching spots on the Twister mat. This game helps to consolidate children's use of 'left' and 'right.'

15 **Model-making** – Use a picture as a guide to building a model.

16 **Tangrams** – of varying degrees of difficulty.

17 **Maps 1** – following directions on a map.

18 **Maps 2** – giving directions for others to follow on a map.

19 **Tessellation 1** – arranging 2D shapes.

20 **Tessellation 2** – arranging and drawing around 2D shapes.

Publishers and suppliers

The following publishers and suppliers have a number of support materials to help children develop spatial awareness skills:

- AVP
- Edu-K – produces books about brain gym
- Formative Fun
- David Fulton publish *Developmental Dyspraxia* by Madeline Portwood
- Galt
- Hope Education
- LDA
- Philip and Tacey
- Rompa
- Select Educational Equipment
- Wesco
- Winslow

(See pages 69–70 for details.)

Listening and attention

Listening is the ability to attend to sounds across a range of stimuli. Attention is the ability to listen carefully and sustain attention. Children with listening and attention difficulties have one of two problems. Either they cannot screen out what is unimportant from what they hear and so listen to everything, or they may not be very skilful at controlling attention and therefore miss large chunks of information.

Children who have difficulties in this area may

- have problems with hearing (make little response to environmental sounds)

- be easily distracted by noise and movement

- tend to daydream and be in a world of their own

- find it hard to focus on one activity at a time

- find it hard to follow instructions – this makes learning and socialising difficult

- often make mistakes because of an inability to attend to detail

- have poor organisational and self-help skills (getting dressed, finding tools for the task)

- avoid tasks that require sustained attention

- be unable to concentrate during tasks involving turn-taking

- have constant movement of hands and feet

- have kinaesthetic strengths and learn better through using concrete materials and practical experiences

- have visual strengths and enjoy learning through using visual materials (charts, maps, videos, demonstrations).

Activities to develop listening and attention skills

1 **Listening to sounds on tape** – (there are commercial materials available, or you can make your own) such as asking the children to listen to a sound and do a specific activity

2 **Sound bingo** – listening to sounds on tape and covering the correct picture.

3 **Sound walk** – listening for different sounds they hear on a walk, then using these to paint a picture or compose a group poem.

4 **Simon says** – listen carefully for specific instructions and then do the actions. (eg. 'Simon says put your hand on your knee').

5 **Shared reading** – using big books to help focus attention on the visual cues.

6 **Circletime activities** – when one child is speaking they could hold a listening shell, which means that everyone else (including the adults) must listen to what they say.

7 **Story tapes** – listening-centre activities can include listening to story tapes interspersed with activities related to the text.

8 **Who am I?** – miming activities can be related to a classroom topic (story characters, occupations, people in the school).

9 **Parachute activities** – children need to listen carefully to the instructions in order to be part of a team activity.

10 **Messages** – ask the children to recall simple messages.

11 **Chinese whispers** – pass an action message round the circle. The last child to receive the message has to perform the action.

12 **Listen and colour** – colour a picture by listening to the instructions.

13 **Listen and draw** – draw a picture by listening to the instructions (there are some published materials for this).

14 **Twenty questions** – allow the children twenty questions to discover the identity of a hidden object related to a class project. Children need to listen carefully to make deductions.

15 **Hot-seating** – one child chooses to be a particular story character and sits in the 'hot seat'. The other children ask questions to discover the identity of the character.

Publishers and suppliers

The following publishers and suppliers have a number of support materials to help children develop listening and attention skills.

- AVP
- Easylearn
- Formative Fun
- Galt
- Hope Education
- Learning Materials
- LDA
- Philip and Tacey
- R-E-M
- Select Educational Equipment
- Wesco
- Winslow

(See pages 69–70 for details.)

Word finding

Word finding is the ability to access vocabulary from the long-term memory. Some children have difficulty in recalling the right word when they need to use it. They often have to describe the word rather than naming it, eg. 'It's hot. You make tea. You put water in it' (kettle). This may be caused by difficulties associating an abstract label with a concrete object. The child may be able to describe the features of something, but not be able to 'find' the correct word in their memory bank.

Children who have difficulties in this area may

- have difficulty naming everyday items

- have difficulty relating words to actions

- have difficulty using age appropriate vocabulary

- substitute words that have a similar meaning (eg. 'cup' for 'mug')

- have kinaesthetic strengths and learn better through using concrete materials and practical experiences

- have visual strengths and enjoy learning through using visual materials (charts, maps, videos, demonstrations).

Activities to develop word finding skills

1 **Action songs** – naming body parts (eg. 'One Finger One Thumb Keeps Moving', 'Head, Shoulders, Knees and Toes').

2 **Classroom labels using symbols** – naming different areas, objects etc.

3 **Draw a person** – name the body parts drawn.

4 **What is it?** – identify classroom items by their use and name them.

5 **Tell me** – in pairs, one child describes an everyday object by function and the other child has to name the object.

6 **Feely bag** – one child has to describe an object by feel to the other children who must try to name the object.

7 **What's missing?** – children look at a picture of a person and draw in the part that is missing, then name it.

8 **Mime time 1** – one child chooses a picture of an object, then mimes how it is used for the others to guess and name.

9 **Naming bingo** – children take turns to pick up a picture card and match it to their baseboard, but they only keep the card if they can name the object on the card.

10 **What am I doing?** – ask the children to name specific actions (eg. clapping, hopping, sitting).

11 **Mime time 2** – one child to choose a picture of an object, then mime how it is used for the others to guess and name.

12 **Listen and name** – ask the children to listen to sounds made by specific objects and then name the object (eg. clock, bell, telephone).

13 **People who work for us** – show the children some object clues and ask them to name the objects and guess who would use them for their job.

14 **Where do I live?** – match an animal to its home and name both animal and home (pictorial).

15 **How many things can you draw and name** – in a bedroom, toy shop, garage, farm etc. Relate this activity to particular areas of the curriculum being taught.

16 **Picture web** – ask the children to draw pictorial reminders around a picture of an item that they have difficulty in remembering.

17 **Pairs** – pictures that have semantic links (eg. knife/fork).

18 **Word for the day** – choose a new concept word, then display it, both pictorially and written, use it in different contexts, relate it to experiential learning and check for recall at the end of each lesson, at the end of the day and at regular intervals throughout the week. This can help reinforce new vocabulary related to class-based topics.

Publishers and suppliers

The following publishers and suppliers have a number of support materials to help children develop word finding skills.

- AVP
- Galt
- Hope Education
- LDA
- Philip and Tacey
- R-E-M
- Select Educational Equipment
- Wesco
- Winslow

(See pages 69–70 for details.)

Semantic knowledge

Semantic knowledge is the ability to understand narrative. This includes the ability to understand the meanings of words in different contexts, as well as a knowledge of the meaning of relationships between words (ie. categories, opposites, synonyms, word association).

Semantics refers to the meanings of words and how they relate to each other. This may be affected by poor auditory memory skills and can have serious implications for children in the classroom. If they cannot retain an understanding of the meaning of new vocabulary, they will have difficulty understanding new concepts and ideas. This will also affect their ability to express their own ideas.

Children with difficulties in this area may

- have word-finding problems
- have difficulty with word classification
- make inappropriate responses to questions, instructions and directions
- have difficulty developing more than a literal understanding of a text
- have a poor short-term auditory memory
- need to be given time to process information
- have kinaesthetic strengths and learn better through using concrete materials and practical experiences
- have visual strengths and enjoy learning through using visual materials (charts, maps, videos, demonstrations).

Activities to develop semantic knowledge

1 **Comparative questions** – eg. 'Is the red ball bigger than the blue ball?'

2 **Opposites** – using everyday objects (eg. thin/fat pencils, old/new shoes).

3 **Sorting** – both real and pictorial items into simple given categories (eg. items we can eat, items we use for writing and drawing).

4 **Classification** – ask children to sort both real and pictorial items into groups, using their own criteria.

5 **Bingo** – simple pictorial categories (establish that each child understands the category on their baseboard before they begin the game).

6 **Odd one out** – ask the children to identify the items that should not be in a specific category and give reasons why.

7 **Which room?** – ask the children to match pictures of objects to specific rooms in the house and give reasons for their choice of room.

8 **Where am I?** – one child chooses a place in the classroom to stand or sit and asks 'Where am I?' The other children have to use a range of prepositions to describe the child's position. (eg. 'You are in front of the teacher's desk.' 'You are next to the blackboard.').

9 **Comparisons** – activities in maths (finding objects that are shorter than, longer than).

10 **Concept opposites** – introduce concept vocabulary within different areas of the curriculum, using visual/concrete materials (eg. hard/soft, full/empty, heavy/light, sweet/sour, rough/smooth).

11 **Homophone pairs, snap, pelmanism** – using pictures and words (eg. see/sea, meet/meat).

12 **Compound word dominoes** – eg. *start*/bed, room/to, day/for, get/pan, cake/hand, bag/*finish*.

13 **Compound picture pairs** – match pictures that form a compound word (eg. foot/ball, butter/fly).

14 **Word families** – collect words that belong to the same category (eg. vegetables, fruit, clothing).

15 **Synonym snap** – this provides an introduction to the use of a simple thesaurus (eg. big/large, small/little).

16 **Synonym families** – the children could make up their own 'happy families' card game, using a simple thesaurus to help them.

Publishers and suppliers

The following publishers and suppliers have a number of support materials to help children develop semantic knowledge.

- AVP
- Galt
- Hope Education
- LDA
- Philip and Tacey
- Select Educational Equipment
- Wesco
- Winslow

(See pages 69–70 for details.)

Grammar (syntax and morphology)

Syntax is about how words are sequenced to convey meaning. This meaning can be changed by rearranging the same words in a different order. (eg. 'I can run fast' changes to 'Can I run fast?'). Morphology refers to the grammar of words and how they are formed. A morpheme represents the smallest unit of meaning in a word. Some children with speech and language impairment have difficulties with using bound morphemes such as -ed, -ing, -s and -es at the ends of words.

Grammar is organising words into sentences, using the correct grammatical word structure. Children who have difficulties with grammar tend to muddle verb tenses. They may find it difficult to pronounce -ed, -ing, and -s on the ends of words and their sentence formation tends to be immature.

Children who have difficulties in this area may

- use immature sentence construction (words may be in the wrong order)
- have difficulty using pronouns correctly
- have difficulty using connectives and articles in both speech and writing
- use word endings (-ed, -ing, -s) incorrectly
- have difficulty with understanding when to use conjunctions and prepositions
- often muddle verb tenses
- have kinaesthetic strengths and learn better through using concrete materials and practical experiences
- have visual strengths and enjoy learning through using visual materials (charts, maps, videos, demonstrations).

Activities to develop grammar skills

1 **Model correct grammar, but don't correct** – eg. if the child says 'I runned to school with my mum,' you might reply 'So you ran to school with your mum. Did you get up late?'

2 **Oral sentence completion** – ask the children to complete open-ended sentences (eg. 'The dog ran into...').

3 **Tell me** – describe objects or pictures orally for others to guess. Child must give sentence clues. (eg. 'It is black. It is very long.').

4 **Sort a sentence** – using known words. The children should recognise that the word with the capital letter starts the sentence and the word with the full stop ends the sentence.

5 **Reorganise simple rhebus sentences** – *Writing with Symbols* could be used for this.

6 **Beginnings and endings** – matching parts of sentences.

7 **Sentence speech bubbles 1** – children to match these to well-known story characters or characters from a core reading scheme.

8 **Written sentence completion** – ask the children to write endings for open-ended sentences (eg. The dog ran into...).

9 **Reorganise sentences** – using given subject/verb/object sentences (eg. The boy/was painting/a picture).

10 **Sentence speech bubbles 2** – children to write these for well-known story characters or characters from a core reading scheme.

11 **Cloze for nouns** – choice of nouns given (A ... was playing football. bus, boy, boat.)

12 **Sentence completion** – using simple information material (eg. 'A baby horse is called a...').

13 **Now and then (verb tenses)** – ask the children to choose sentences that can be placed on the 'now' or 'then' boards. (eg. The girl walked to school. The girl is walking to school.)

14 **Did you know?** – ask the children to write some simple sentence information facts.

15 **Verb change** – ask the children to change a verb that has been repeated in a passage.

16 **Who did that?** – Ask the children to identify pronouns with people in a text.

17 **Cloze** – for verbs, adjectives and adverbs.

Publishers and suppliers

The following publishers and suppliers have a number of support materials to help children develop grammar skills.

- Addison Wesley Longman produces *Breakthrough to Literacy*
- AVP
- Crossbow Educational
- Easylearn
- Galt
- Hope Education
- Hopscotch Educational Publishing
- Hilda King Educational
- Learning Materials
- LDA
- Philip and Tacey

- R-E-M
- Select Educational Equipment
- Wesco
- Widgit Software produces *Writing with Symbols*
- Winslow

(See pages 69–70 for details.)

Social communication (pragmatics)

Pragmatics refers to the ability to communicate in social situations. Some children have difficulty in understanding how to use language in a range of different social situations and can make very inappropriate remarks.

Children who have difficulties in this area may

- have problems with taking turns in a conversation or in games
- be unable to change the style of conversation to suit the listener
- be unable to interpret tone of voice in others
- have difficulty interpreting non-verbal communication (ie. facial expression, gestures)
- have difficulty keeping to the topic of a conversation
- have problems with judging the amount of previous knowledge that the listener has when relating information
- have difficulty understanding other points of view
- have strengths in a specific area of the curriculum
- have a particular interest or hobby which can sometimes act as a stimulus to learning
- have a good memory for rote learning.

Activities to develop social communication skills

1 **Role play** – adults and other children to model social situations at home, shopping etc.

2 **Puppets** – adults and other children to model social situations through puppet plays and stories.

3 **Take part** – children with social communication difficulties to be encouraged to take an active part in both role play and puppet activities after watching modelled situations.

4 **Tell me** – ask the children to talk about personal experiences to the class. Subtle adult questioning should ensure that a child keeps to the topic and gives relevant background information.

5 **Making faces** – miming activities, specifically teaching children how to show feelings through facial expression. This could be part of miming scenes from well-known stories (eg. the three little pigs being frightened of the wolf).

6 **Board games** – these involve turn-taking.

7 **Parachute games** – these involve collaboration and need to be introduced gradually until the children can work as a team.

8 **Circletime** – gives opportunities to develop the ability to listen to other children's points of view, even if they have difficulty in understanding them.

9 **Reactions** – ask the children to choose a reaction, from a choice of three, to a particular social situation. Then talk about the possible consequences of each reaction.

10 **Speech bubbles** – using well-known story characters. Read the children a scene from the story and then ask them to write, in the speech bubble, what the character might say at the end of the scene.

11 **Just a minute** – ask the children to talk about a particular subject for one minute. This is good practice at keeping to the topic.

12 **Social stories** – a well-researched and published approach to help children cope with certain social situations that they find difficult.

13 **Comic strip conversations** – a well-researched and published approach to help children cope with making choices in certain social situations.

Publishers and suppliers

The following publishers and suppliers have a number of support materials to help children develop social communication skills.

- Formative Fun
- Galt
- Hope Education
- LDA
- Philip and Tacey
- Select Educational Equipment
- Wesco
- Winslow supplies *Social Stories* and *Comic Strip Conversations*

(See pages 69–70 for details.)

Gross motor skills

Gross motor skills are the movements of the large muscles of the body. These skills involve the coordinated effort of the large muscle groups. Children with some medical conditions have poor or delayed gross motor skills, which affects balance and motor planning.

Children who have difficulties in this area may have

- difficulty throwing and catching a ball
- balance problems when hopping and jumping
- balance problems when using apparatus in gymnastics
- balance problems when riding a bike
- low muscle tone
- good auditory memory skills
- confidence as speakers and listeners
- good verbal comprehension skills.

Activities to develop gross motor skills

All these activities are general ones that can be used to develop gross motor coordination for most children in your class. However, some children may need a much more specific programme of activities. Occupational therapists and physiotherapists will need to assess the children's needs and advise on particular gross motor activities to address each child's specific difficulties.

1 **Dodgems** – ask the children to run around in different directions, making sure that they do not bump into each other. They need to dodge out of the way of each other. You can make this game more difficult by calling out 'Change' so that the children have to change direction.

2 **Stone cold** – give each child a number, then ask them all to run around in different directions. If their number is called they have to stand still like a statue until the next number is called when they can move again.

3 **Stepping stones** – using small hoops as stepping stones, ask the children to 'cross the water' by jumping from one to the other without falling in the 'water'.

4 **Hopscotch** – children can jump to begin with until they feel confident with hopping.

5 **Parachute games** – ones that use the large muscle movements.

6 **Climbing activities** – using a range of large apparatus.

7 **Balancing activities** – using a range of both small and large apparatus.

8 **Brain gym** – some of the suggested activities involve the coordinated movement of some of the large muscles.

9 **Bean bag activities** – a range of team games involving throwing bean bags at a target, or putting bean bags into a bucket, hoop etc., or games involving kicking or throwing

10 **Ball games** – a range of games involving rolling, kicking, throwing and catching.

11 **Batting activities** – a range of games involving the use of bats, sticks or racquets. These could be
    - dribbling a ball around objects using a hockey stick
    - timing how long the children can keep a ball in the air by batting it
    - putting a ball into a specific position, using a putter or a hockey stick
    - paired games as in table tennis, racquet ball and short tennis
    - team games as in rounders, cricket and hockey.

12 **Skipping activities** – individual and group skipping games (eg. 'Salt, Mustard, Vinegar, Pepper').

Publishers and suppliers

The following publishers and suppliers have a number of support materials to help children develop gross motor skills.

- Edu-K – produces books about brain gym
- Formative Fun
- David Fulton publish *Developmental Dyspraxia* by Madeline Portwood
- Galt
- Hope Education
- LDA
- Philip and Tacey
- Rompa
- Select Educational Equipment
- Wesco

(See pages 69–70 for details.)

Fine motor skills

This is the ability to use the smaller muscles in the body for precise tasks, such as writing, drawing, sewing, using scissors, tying shoelaces etc. Many school activities involve fine motor skills.

Children with difficulties in this area may have

- poor eye–hand coordination
- poor manipulative skills
- immature drawing skills
- poor handwriting and presentation skills
- some perceptual difficulties
- good auditory memory skills
- confidence as speakers and listeners
- good verbal comprehension skills
- strengths in verbal and non-verbal reasoning
- enjoyment in using multisensory strategies when learning.

Activities to develop fine motor skills

All these activities are general ones that can be used to develop fine motor skills for most children in your class. However, some children may need a much more specific programme of activities. Occupational therapists and physiotherapists will need to assess individual children's needs and advise on particular fine motor activities to address their specific difficulties.

1 **Take a line for a walk** – see how long the pencil can stay on the paper.
2 **Sorting** – small objects such as paper clips, screws, bolts, buttons etc.
3 **Clipping things together** – using pegs, paper clips etc.
4 **Dressing up activities** – involving the use of clothing fasteners such as buttons, zippers and laces.
5 **Post-a-shape** – matching shapes to the correct opening.
6 **Bead threading** – copy the pattern.
7 **Tracking and maze activities**.
8 **Cutting and pasting** – patterns, pictures, classification activities, project scrapbooks.
9 **Tracing** – lines, shapes and simple pictures.
10 **Copy writing patterns 1** – using coloured sand.
11 **Copy writing patterns 2** – using chalk.
12 **Colouring patterns and pictures** – using different media.

13 **Dot-to-dot pictures** – using numbers and the alphabet.
14 **Line-links** – following the line from one end to the other (eg. mouse to the cheese).
15 **Modelling** – with clay, Plasticine etc.
16 **Painting and printing** – using different sized brushes and different types of printing materials.
17 **Jigsaw puzzles** – starting with simple peg puzzles with pictures and shapes that need to be slotted into the correct space, then introducing traditional puzzles of varying degrees of difficulty.
18 **Peg boards** – these can be used to make simple or more complex patterns.
19 **Building blocks** – start with larger wooden ones if possible and then introduce smaller ones.
20 **Constructional apparatus** – of varying degrees of difficulty (eg. Duplo, Lego).
21 **Jacks or marbles** – children learn to control fine motor movements with these games.
22 **Computer-aided picture and design activities**.
23 **Sewing activities**.
24 **Finger puppets**.
25 **Construction activities** – involving the use of plastic nuts, bolts and screws.
26 **Musical instruments** – playing as wide a range as available.

Publishers and suppliers

The following publishers and suppliers have a number of support materials to help children develop fine motor skills.

- AVP
- Formative Fun
- David Fulton publish *Developmental Dyspraxia* by Madeline Portwood
- Galt
- Hope Education
- LDA
- Philip and Tacey
- R-E-M
- Rompa
- Select Educational Equipment
- Wesco

(See pages 69–70 for details.)

Learning difficulties grid

The photocopiable grid on page 72 provides a useful method of keeping track of the needs of the SEN children in a particular year-group or class. It can be filled in by the SEN coordinator for the teachers, either at transfer between classes or during the year, or it can be an ongoing record for the class teachers themselves to keep.

The purpose of the grid is to provide an overview of the learning difficulties experienced across a group of children, to see what specific support they each need and how they might be grouped for different activities. Most of the skills or concepts are those addressed in this chapter.

We have added a row for emotional and behavioural difficulties. Usually such problems are noted in children as an effect of their learning difficulty and their resulting frustrations and low self-esteem. However, there are occasions (such as family break-ups) when emotional and behavioural problems are the cause of the child having learning difficulties and are therefore, in themselves, barriers to learning for a time.

In order to demonstrate how the photocopiable grid can be used, we have also given you an example on page 71. You can see at a glance which children it would be appropriate to group together to do some auditory activities, for example, or who might benefit from a practical session to increase fine motor skills together.

Suppliers and publishers details

Addison Wesley Longman
Edinburgh Gate
Harlow
Essex CM20 2JE
Tel: 01279 623367

AVP
School Hill Centre
Chepstow
Monmouthshire NP16 5PH
Tel: 01291 625439
www.avp.co.uk

Buzan Centres Ltd
54 Parkstone Road
Poole
Dorset BH15 2PG.
Tel: 01202 674676
www.Mind-Map.com

Crossbow Educational
41 Sawpit Lane
Brocton
Staffordshire ST17 0TE
Tel: 01785 660902
www.crossboweducation.com

Easylearn
Trent House
Fiskerton
Southwell NG25 0UH
Tel: 01636 830240
www.easylearn.co.uk

Edu-K (Educational Kinesiology Foundation)
12 Golders Rise
London NW4 2HR
Tel: 020 8202 3141
www.braingym.org.uk

Egon Publishers
Royston Road
Baldock
Hertfordshire SG7 6NW
Tel: 01462 894 498
www.egon.co.uk

Formative Fun
Education House
Horn Park Business Centre
Broadwindsor Road
Beaminster DT8 3PT
Tel: 01308 868999
www.formative-fun.com

David Fulton Publishers
The Chiswick Centre
414 Chiswick High Road
London W4 5TF
Tel: 020 8996 3610
www.fultonpublishers.

Galt Educational and Pre-school
Johnsonbrook Road
Hyde
Cheshire SK1 4QT
Tel: 08451 20 30 05
www.galt-educational.co.uk

HELP Educational Games
PO Box 412
Amersham
Buckinghamshire HP7 9WB
Tel: 01494 765261
www.helpgames.co.uk

Hilda King Educational
Ashwells
Manor Drive
Penn
High Wycombe
Buckinghamshire
Tel: 01494 813947
www.hildaking.clara.net

Hope Education
Hyde Buildings
Ashton Road
Cheshire SK14 4SH
Tel: 08451 202055
www.hope-education.co.uk

Hopscotch Educational Publishing Ltd
29 Waterloo Place
Leamington Spa
Warwickshire CV32 5LA
Tel: 01926 744227
www.hopscotchbooks.com

Learning Materials Ltd
Dixon Street
Wolverhampton WV2 2BX
Tel: 01902 454026
www.learning.materials.btinternet.co.uk

LDA
Duke Street
Wisbech
Cambridgeshire PE13 2AE
Tel: 01945 463441
www.LDAlearning.com

Philip and Tacey Ltd
North Way
Andover
Hampshire SP10 5BA
Tel: 01264 332171
www.philipandtacey.co.uk

The Psychological Corporation (Harcourt)
Halley Court
Jordan Hill
Oxford OX2 8EJ
Tel: 01865 888 188
www.tpc-international.com

R-E-M (Basic Skills and Special Needs catalogue)
Great Western House
Langport
Somerset TA10 9YU
Tel: 01458 254 700
www.r-e-m.co.uk

Rompa
Goyt Side Road
Chesterfield
Derbyshire S40 2PH
Tel: 0800 056 2323
www.rompa.com

Select Educational Equipment
Unit 4, Arcadia Park
Towers Business Park
Wheelhouse Road
Rugeley
Staffordshire WS15 1UZ
Tel: 01889 578 333
www.selecteducationalequipment.co.uk

Taskmaster Ltd
Morris Road
Leicester LE2 6BR
Tel: 0116 270 4286
www.taskmasteronline.co.uk

Thrass (UK) Limited
Units 1–3 Tarvin Sands
Barrow Lane
Tarvin
Chester CH3 8JF
Tel: 01829 741413
www.thrass.co.uk

WESCO
114 Highfields Road
Witham
Essex CM8 2HH
Tel: 01376 503590
www.wesco-group.com

Whurr Publications Ltd
19b Compton Terrace
London N1 2UN
Tel: 020 7359 5979
www.whurr.co.uk

Widgit Software
124 Cambridge Science Park
Milton Road
Cambridge CB4 0ZS
Tel: 01223 425558
www.widgit.com

Winslow Press Ltd (Education and Special Needs)
Telford Road
Bicester
Oxfordshire OX26 4LQ
Telephone: 01869 244644
www.winslow-press.co.uk

SEN children's principle areas of learning difficulty

Year group 4

Learning difficulties	Names											
	R.S.	A.R.	J.C.	M.D.	K.L.	S.L.	M.S.	L.G				
Auditory discrimination		✓										
Auditory memory	✓	✓	✓		✓	✓	✓					
Fine motor	✓			✓	✓	✓						
Grammar (syntax and morphology			✓				✓					
Gross motor				✓								
Listening and attention	✓	✓			✓	✓	✓					
Phonological awareness		✓			✓	✓	✓					
Physical disability				✓								
Semantic knowledge			✓				✓					
Sensory impairment				✓								
Social communication	✓						✓					
Spatial awareness	✓			✓	✓							
Verbal comprehension			✓				✓					
Visual discrimination				✓								
Visual memory	✓			✓								
Visual perception	✓			✓								
Word finding	✓						✓					
Emotional/behavioural								✓				

SEN children's principle areas of learning difficulty

Year group

Learning difficulties	Names										
Auditory discrimination											
Auditory memory											
Fine motor											
Grammar (syntax and morphology											
Gross motor											
Listening and attention											
Phonological awareness											
Physical disability											
Semantic knowledge											
Sensory impairment											
Social communication											
Spatial awareness											
Verbal comprehension											
Visual discrimination											
Visual memory											
Visual perception											
Word finding											
Emotional/behavioural											

CHAPTER 5
Teaching assistants

Teaching assistants (TAs) have a vital role to play in supporting children with special needs in school and you will work closely with them on a day-to-day basis. This chapter looks in detail at that role and at your involvement in it as SEN coordinator. TAs now have opportunities for career progression and you may also have a wider management responsibility for them, from recruitment to induction to career development. This chapter also considers these aspects of the SEN coordinator's work.

Who are teaching assistants?

Supporting the Teaching Assistant – A Good Practice Guide tells us that

> 'The term "teaching assistant" (TA) is the government's preferred generic term of reference for all those in paid employment in support of teachers in primary, special and secondary schools. That includes those with a general role and others with specific responsibilities for a child, subject area or age group. The term captures the essential "active ingredient" of their work; in particular it acknowledges the contribution which well-trained and well-managed assistants can make to the teaching and learning process and to pupil achievement."
> (DfES, 2000 – page 4)

Throughout this chapter, we will use the title teaching assistant (TA) for the role, as defined above. However, we also recognise that many schools and LEAs still refer to TAs by a range of other job titles, perhaps relating to specific areas of the role. The title learning support assistant (LSA) continues to be a much-used and appropriate title for some TAs, working with individuals or small groups on a regular basis. The 2001 SEN Code of Practice supports the continuing use of the title LSA and defines it as

> '...a widely used job title for an assistant providing in-school support for pupils with special educational needs and/or disabilities. An LSA will normally work with a particular pupil or pupils providing close support to the individual pupil and assistance to those responsible for teaching him/her. Some assistants specialising in SEN may also be known by titles other than LSA as these matters are decided locally. LSAs are one of a group of assistants coming within the broader DfES classification of "teaching assistant"'.'
> (DfES, 2001 – glossary)

Where did the role of teaching assistant originate?

The role of the TA expanded hugely through the 1990s and the early part of the new century. Until the late eighties, additional adults employed to work in classrooms were only seen in Reception classes. They were usually given the lowly title of welfare assistant or ancillary helper and paid to wash paintpots, tie shoelaces, cut paper, sharpen pencils, find dry knickers and administer rudimentary first aid. Everybody in the school community overlooked them, except those lucky teachers in whose classrooms these assistants worked.

A few forward-looking class teachers realised the potential of their assistants and saw the benefits for themselves and their pupils of creating a collaborative partnership with their assistants. With these teachers, classroom assistants flourished and began to pave the way for higher status, greater support for teaching and more active participation in children's learning.

Throughout the nineties, attitudes changed and the pile of documents supporting the enhancement of the roles of support staff in schools grew. More and more teachers were able to benefit from having the help of skilled and increasingly valuable assistants for more sustained and regular periods of time, working with individuals or groups and with specific objectives. Often, with increasing inclusion, these assistants were attached to individual SEN children, or perhaps SEN groups, on a daily basis. As they came to know their charges better and became more involved in their day-to-day learning, attainment and progress, so their observations turned into assessments and they began to be valued contributors to IEPs and reviews.

The current climate for teaching assistants

Recent developments and government initiatives are revolutionising the roles and the status of TAs. They are now recognised as valued professionals who have a clear and very important place in supporting the work of the children, the teachers and the school as a whole.

In 2002, Ofsted issued a brief evaluation entitled *Teaching Assistants in Primary Schools*, which highlighted the immense contribution made by many TAs in all types of schools.

> 'Evidence from Ofsted section 10 inspections shows that the quality of teaching in lessons with teaching assistants is better than in lessons without them.' (Ofsted, 2002)

In addition to supporting teachers and children in classrooms, Ofsted found that

> 'Teaching assistants contribute to the wider life of a school by giving generously of their time and talents. They often have an informal but influential pastoral role, and provide continuity between classes for both pupils and teachers.' (Ofsted, 2002)

Supporting the Teaching Assistant praises

> '...the tremendous contribution well-managed and well-trained teaching assistants can make in driving up standards in schools.' (DfES, 2000 – foreword)

In this document, the DfES announced a programme of additional recruitment, effective training and greater clarity over role and qualifications pathways for TAs. To ensure that all of this takes place within the desired timescale, the government has increased funding to schools, year by year. This increased funding is part of the government's drive to reform schools and the document itself provides a foundation for revolutionising the way teachers work with support staff in schools 'to build learning teams that help pupils realise their potential.'

The *National Occupational Standards for Teaching/ Classroom Assistants* were introduced in April 2001 to 'represent best practice expectations about the role and responsibilities of teaching/classroom assistants.' (LGNTO, 2001 – preface) We will look at these standards in some detail later in this chapter.

To summarise, the current position is that schools are being given increased levels of funding to enable them to recruit and train additional TAs. New,

award-bearing routes for training and development are being created and innovative styles of working are being trialled in targeted schools across the country.

Roles and responsibilities

There are a number of responsibilities that are part of every TA's role, added to which will be individual and specific duties, identified and agreed between the TA and their line manager, which may be you. The individual role and responsibilities of each TA will need to be set out in a job description, and we will look at this later in the chapter. The TA's duties may need to be amended over time, to meet changes in the demands placed on schools or the needs of children and teachers.

Most TAs, whether or not they are attached to individual children, will spend the majority of their time in classrooms with groups of children, supporting their learning. They may also have other duties in support of the class teacher, the SEN coordinator, the whole staff or the whole school. TAs may also have specific and specialised skills, which should be deployed creatively.

Although the list of activities in the box opposite is long, it is by no means exhaustive. As *Supporting the Teaching Assistant* states

> '...each school has its own character and needs, and managers must think through how to gain the best from deploying TAs according to their school's needs and plans.' (DfES, 2000 – p4)

Your school will probably have identified one of the most experienced TAs to lead and coordinate the work of the whole team of TAs. You and the headteacher will need to work closely with this team leader in order to achieve optimum provision and to encourage partnership with all staff groups.

Supporting the Teaching Assistant also states that

> 'The essence of the successful deployment of TAs lies in understanding the nature of the support that they can provide. This can be divided into four strands.
> - Support for the pupil.
> - Support for the teacher.
> - Support for the curriculum.
> - Support for the school.' (DfES, 2000 – p8)

What do TAs do?

TAs may be asked or may volunteer to undertake a wide variety of tasks, including such activities as

- supporting the learning of individuals or groups of children in the classroom or elsewhere in the school
- motivating and encouraging children to give of their best in a range of situations
- managing the learning and behaviour of an individual or group of children
- preparing or amending teaching materials and organising resources
- participating in the teaching or support of the whole class, in partnership with, at the direction of or under the supervision of the class-teacher
- looking after the majority of the class while the teacher works with a group, such as the SEN children
- providing observation and assessment feedback to the class teacher and the SEN coordinator
- contributing to the planning of lessons and study units
- meeting or liaising with outside agencies, professionals or outreach
- participating in reviews, target-setting and IEP writing
- hearing children read as a reading mentor
- providing other forms of mentor support, such as informal counselling of children, with the parents' agreement
- leading extra-curricular activities
- supervising break-times and leading playground games
- providing welfare support for the staff (such as refreshments during wet playtimes)
- coordinating and/or administering first aid
- making Health and Safety checks
- ordering materials
- undertaking photocopying, book-making and other administrative or routine tasks
- assisting the headteacher and SEN coordinator with higher-level managerial activities
- mounting and putting up wall displays around the school
- providing ICT support and perhaps technical backup
- managing a wildlife garden or pets' corner
- maintaining the school library or music room
- helping with drama productions and performances.

Support for the child

This means supporting the learning and inclusion of those children for whom the TA has direct responsibility and all children with whom she or he comes into contact.

Support for the teacher

This involves carrying out tasks such as escorting or supervising groups of children, carrying out routine tasks, or supporting and assessing children's work.

Support for the curriculum

Some TAs support children specifically in literacy or numeracy lessons, but many TAs are likely to work across the whole curriculum, giving support in all subjects, including PE and ICT.

Support for the school

TAs are part of the whole school team. This means translating school policies into practice and furthering the ethos and development of the whole school.

These four strands of TA support are not separate but interdependent. The TA will be fulfilling one or more of these aims at all times in support of the school. But the school also has a responsibility to support its TAs

> '...in fulfilling the expectations of the role ... management support should enable them to perform the job to the best of their abilities, and they should be encouraged to develop their skills and potential. Clearly, this view of two-way support requires the close cooperation of class teachers with whom TAs work.'
> (DfES, 2000 – p8)

The Management, Role and Training of Learning Support Assistants, a University of Manchester survey, found that effective work by TAs

- 'fosters the participation of pupils in the social and academic processes of a school
- seeks to enable pupils to become more independent learners
- helps to raise standards of achievement for all pupils.' (1999)

Effective day-to-day activities

As *Supporting the Teaching Assistant* suggests, these aspects of good practice can be further subdivided into effective day-to-day activities.

1 Fostering the participation of pupils in social and academic processes

This will include

- supervising and assisting small groups of children in activities set by teachers

- developing children's social skills
- implementing behaviour management policies
- spotting early signs of bullying and disruptive behaviour
- helping the inclusion of all children
- keeping children on task.

2 Seeking to enable pupils to become more independent learners

This will include

- showing interest
- assisting individuals in educational tasks
- freeing up the teacher to work with groups
- working with outside agencies
- modelling good practice
- assisting children with physical needs.

3 Helping to raise standards of achievement of all pupils

This will include

- being involved at whole-class level
- helping implement lesson plans
- making possible more ambitious learning activities
- providing support for the Literacy and Numeracy Strategies
- providing feedback to teachers
- preparing classroom materials.

The National Standards are 'the benchmarks of good practice'. They provide a comprehensive framework for the role and deployment of TAs, built on agreed values and principles, which are

- working in partnership with the teacher
- working within statutory and organisational frameworks
- supporting inclusion
- equality of opportunity
- anti-discrimination
- celebrating diversity
- promoting independence
- confidentiality
- continuing professional development.

The National Standards are presented in the form of units of competence, which are in turn the building blocks for the National Vocational Qualifications (NVQs) for TAs. This correlation will be looked at further, later in this chapter.

Each National Standards unit of competence sets out the scope of the particular unit and is supported by

- a unit summary
- a glossary of terms
- two or more standards
- a set of performance indicators
- a specified knowledge base.

Recruiting teaching assistants

Whilst recruitment and appointment is generally the task of the headteacher and governors of the school, as SEN coordinator, you may well be asked to participate in the selection process for SEN TAs. Two important documents you will have to contribute to are the person specification and the job description.

Person specification

The first part of this process is deciding on the kind of person you are looking for. A number of factors will need to be taken into consideration to arrive at your person specification, including the particular needs of the child or children with whom the TA will be expected to work, the requirements of the staff and the activities of the school.

First, you will need to think about the desirable qualities and skills of the ideal person to fill this post. Optimum qualities will almost certainly include (not in any particular order)

- flexibility
- initiative
- rapport with children
- patience, calmness and understanding
- ability to work in a team
- willingness to train and learn
- a balance of firmness and fairness
- alertness
- tact and sensitivity
- confidentiality
- common-sense and maturity
- a sense of humour

Flexibility

However much we might wish that everything always went according to plan, schools are peopled by children who are often anything but predictable. This, together with the unexpected events caused by old plumbing and heating systems, electricity cuts, fallen trees, flooded playgrounds, leaking roofs, broken down buses and epidemics, not to mention the weather, can wreak havoc with the best laid plans. At times like these, adaptable TAs can make all the difference as to whether a memorable experience is fun-filled or disastrous!

Initiative

With a class of thirty or more children, across a wide range of abilities and needs, the most talented teacher will not be able to attend to every child or meet every demand at the same time. This is where the TA with initiative will see something that needs to be done or a child who needs some immediate attention and quietly get on and do it, without the teacher missing a beat or the child(ren) having time to build up any frustration or anxiety.

Rapport with children

This may seem obvious, but it is a real talent for an unfamiliar adult to be able to make an immediate bond with a group of children. This may be difficult to identify in a CV or a letter of application, but it can be noted through observation when taking the prospective candidate on a tour of the school. If time allows, a really good way to judge the quality of the applicant's relationships with children will be to suggest they come and spend some time in a classroom before the interviews.

Patience, calmness and understanding

Once again, these qualities would seem to be a given, but some SEN children will try the patience and understanding of the most saintly TA on a daily basis. Children do not respond well to highly-strung adults in learning situations, so a TA needs to be able to remain unflappable, no matter what.

Team-ability

TAs must not only be able to work alongside class teachers and as part of a busy and effective team, but they must be able to enjoy working with others. They must be able to see their role as part of a larger whole and they must be willing to accept guidance and direction, not only from their line managers, but also from each other when needs dictate the team to work as one unit.

Willingness to train and learn

While most schools have, in recent years, built up their own programmes of training and development for TAs, there is now a wide range of training available outside the school, which gives new opportunities for professional development and career progression. We cannot expect, nor should

we, that every TA will want to gain qualifications at ever increasing levels, but willingness to learn is an essential pre-requisite of the post in today's learning community.

A balance of firmness and fairness

This is a natural attribute which it is difficult to cultivate from scratch. Children will soon suss out the chinks in any new TA's armour, especially if they are inconsistent or wavering in their approach. Like any good teacher, TAs need to start as they mean to go on and be firm but fair at all times.

Alertness

Every good TA will have good listening and observational skills. They will be able to take in new information, whether seen or heard, planned or unexpected, very quickly and will be able to translate this into effective action.

Tact and sensitivity

There will be many occasions when the TA may be required to deal with difficult situations. A child may confide in them about a situation in the home, a parent may quiz them on the 'problems' of another child in the school, or the teacher in whose class they are working may say or do something they feel to be inappropriate. Whatever the occasion, the TA will need to be circumspect, to understand the balance between respecting confidentiality and safeguarding the well-being of a child and to know when it is appropriate to raise the matter with their line manager or with the school's child protection officer.

Confidentiality

If the TA is a member of the local community, as most are, they will know many of the families whose children attend the school and with whom they may work. Indeed, they will probably socialise regularly with some of the parents. They will need to be able to keep these two areas of their life completely separate and take on a professional attitude to the job.

Common-sense and maturity

While most qualities can be developed and most skills can be learned on the job or in training, anyone who works in a school must possess an instinctive understanding of what is needed in schools. They must be able not only to read and take on board the school's policies, for example, but also to be able to interpret them and understand the need for having them in the first place. From this starting point, TAs will be ready to learn from the induction process and to fulfil their role as effectively as possible.

A sense of humour

Anyone who works in a school must have a genuine sense of humour, to offset all the stresses and strains of the role, not to mention ever increasing expectations. Seemingly surreal events happen on a daily basis in schools, and being able to see the funny side of such situations lightens the load and helps everyone to cope with all the more demanding aspects of school life.

In addition to these qualities, and perhaps others that your school has identified, it will be useful if the chosen candidate has had training in appropriate skills, such as first aid or ICT and has a reasonable level of literacy and numeracy skills. Of course, if your primary requirement is for someone to provide physical care for a severely disabled child, then these acquired skills will be of secondary importance to the special kinds of qualities they will need in this role. Your person specification will reflect these individual circumstances.

Job description

Once you have identified the required skills and qualities for the person specification, you will now be in a position to put together a job description for the TA's post. There are a number of generic formats available on which to base your own TAs' job descriptions, but you may feel that none of them quite distils what you have in mind for your school. Then there is the problem of keeping pace with all the latest developments and changes in expectations of TAs.

Supporting the Teaching Assistant includes a simple pro forma which could provide you with a very useful starting point, based simply on purpose, responsibilities and duties in the four support categories (pupils, teachers, school and curriculum). Alternatively, you might choose to use the National Standards as a framework, selecting the units of competence which best match the job role and using these to devise a relevant job description.

If you need to put together from scratch a generic job description appropriate to your school, you might like to use the example on the opposite page as a model to adapt for this purpose.

Fine-tuning the job description

Once the TA is in post, it is advisable to consult them regarding any necessary amendments to their job description, to include everything they are actually required to do and to omit any irrelevant statements. Indeed, with teamwork and cooperation in mind, this would be a really useful opportunity for the class teacher and the TA to work together, defining the details of the post.

Where a TA has a specific responsibility for an individual child or children, the job description should make clear reference to this responsibility and it should specify to what extent, if any, the TA is also expected to support the teaching and learning of other children in the class.

The clearer and more individualised a job description is, the more effective it will be in both the performance management and professional development processes.

Induction of teaching assistants

All new staff need to take part in an induction process, which introduces them to the physical environment of the school, the people in it, the routines and policies, the times and order of things and the resources available. Two essential elements in the induction process are the mentor and the induction pack or staff handbook.

The mentor

A new TA isn't going to learn everything she or he needs to know by accident. They need a sympathetic mentor who will apprise them of all the essential information, some of which may be confidential, especially if it is about a particular SEN child with whom they will be working. This mentor could be anybody on the staff who is willing to support new appointees as they take up their post. It could be the headteacher or deputy, or a class teacher or the administration officer. However, it will probably be most sensible for a senior TA to take on this role for every newly appointed TA. In this way, the induction process can be planned and tailored for the needs of TAs.

As part of the induction process, the mentor should find out about the new TA's strengths and interests and any special skills she or he may have, such as expertise in ICT, being a trained football coach or playing chess. These skills and interests could be noted down to start off the new TA's professional development file.

Induction pack

The mentor will have identified the most important information, to be passed on first and will show the new TA the where, what, when and how of the job.

Job description for a teaching assistant

NAME .... GRADE ....

RESPONSIBLE TO ....

Main purpose of the job

To work alongside the teachers of Years 5 and 6, supporting children in their learning across the curriculum, under the guidance of the class teacher.

Duties and responsibilities

Support for children

- Support children during learning activities.
- Support the maintenance of child safety and security.
- Establish and maintain relationships with individual children and groups.
- Promote children's social and emotional development.
- Provide support for EAL children.
- Support children with communication difficulties.
- Support children with learning difficulties.
- Support children with behavioural, emotional and social development needs.
- Provide support for children with sensory or physical impairment.

Support for teachers

- Contribute to the planning and evaluation of learning activities.
- Contribute to maintaining children's records.
- Observe and report on children's performance.
- Assist in preparing and maintaining the learning environment.
- Contribute to the management of children's behaviour.

Support for the school

- Support the development of effective work teams.
- Develop and maintain working relationships with other professionals.
- Liaise effectively with parents.

Support for the curriculum

- Support the use of ICT in the classroom.
- Help children to develop their literacy skills.
- Help children to develop their numeracy skills.
- Help children to access the curriculum.

Additional and specific tasks

- Support a child in Year 5 with Asperger syndrome every morning.
- Liaise with the other TA supporting this child in the afternoons.
- Meet daily with the class teacher for five minutes before school to keep each other up to date on the needs and progress of this child.
- Act as reading mentor for a small group of children with reading delay in Year 5.
- Take part in the administration of first aid on a rota basis.
- Run an extra-curricular activity during the Friday afternoon 'golden time'.

Training and development

- Be prepared to attend courses or undertake relevant training.
- Take part in the school's performance development process, setting targets for development and reviewing achievements.

If there is a specially designed (and not too long-winded) induction pack, this will be very useful. It will take a long time for the new TA to learn the names of the teachers and assistants with whom they will be working most closely, let alone everyone in the school. It helps to have names written down and where these people are based. It helps even more if there are photographs next to the names.

It is important for this pack to include the protocols of the job – for example, where do you leave the money to pay for a telephone call? All this, and more, should be set out in the induction pack, together with a summary list of resources and where they are to be found. If an induction pack isn't available, then the staff handbook will be the next best thing, as long as it is up-to-date. The mentor will need to ensure that the TA is introduced straight away to the most important aspects.

- **Job description** – if they don't already have it, this will be a crucial document for them to receive, explaining their role and responsibilities in the school.

- **Names and roles** – of other members of the teaching staff and TA teams, where they are based and who to go to for specific requirements.
- **Year groups as classes** – in other words, the class titles and who is in them.
- **The aims of the school and its mission statement** – an outline of what the school is about and what its guiding principles are.
- **Routines and timetables** – who does what, when and where.
- **Playtime and lunchtime arrangements** – what role do the TAs play and do they share any responsibilities, such as providing refreshments or administering first aid.
- **School calendar** – key dates and events for the term.
- **Selected policy documents** – this will depend on the new TA's role, but will almost certainly include copies of the behaviour policy, the SEN policy, the Equal Opportunities policy and the Health and Safety policy.

Formal induction training

Induction doesn't need to stop after the first week in post. It should be an ongoing process and could include some more formal training, such as the DfES's specially designed induction programme, which leads into the NVQ qualifications. The Local Government National Training Organisation (LGNTO) has produced some diagrams mapping the links between the induction materials and the NVQs and also between the induction materials and the National Standards. These clear and helpful mapping grids, together with the induction training materials can be downloaded from the LGNTO website www.lgnto.gov.uk

Ofsted's evaluation of the work of TAs in primary schools found that

> 'Where schools have taken part in the DfES Induction Training, the confidence and competence of Teaching Assistants, and the way they are managed in schools, have all improved.' (Ofsted, 2002)

Following the formal induction course, TAs will be encouraged to compile a portfolio of evidence which may then be used to contribute to the NVQ, should they wish to embark on this. They will also be encouraged to keep a journal or reflective diary of their experiences and responses, which could in turn feed into their professional development and performance management.

Professional development

As SEN coordinator, you will probably be line-managing a number of TAs. Some may support individual children, while others may work with small groups or in other roles. All your TAs will bring to their work a variety of skills, expertise and experience. Some will be interested in developing very specific areas of their expertise, others will be interested in curriculum development and some may wish to gain qualifications which could either enhance their career as a higher level TA, or which could enable them to move on into teacher training. Whatever their needs and aspirations, it is important that they each feel part of the team. They need to be shown that their skills are valued and that any training they may choose to undertake is not just for themselves, but is also an important part of the 'big picture' for the school.

There is no doubt that the training and development of TAs is money well spent. It should be seen as an investment for the school and its children. In its consultation document *Developing the Role of School Support Staff*, the DfES stated that

> 'With the right training and supervision, as well as sufficient numbers, support staff can release significant amounts of time for teachers and headteachers to focus on their core professional role, improving standards of teaching and learning ... Increased numbers of better trained support staff will in their own right enrich the experience of pupils.' (2002, Executive summary)

The government has declared its intention to extend training opportunities for TAs by

- extending the scope and range of induction training
- encouraging the development of progression routes (examined later in more detail)
- introducing standards for higher-level TA roles
- developing smoother progression routes to Qualified Teacher Status for TAs who wish to train as teachers
- developing higher-level specialist roles
- providing additional funding to develop and implement new training provision.

Whether they focus on in-school training and development or choose to embark on additional, formal training, TAs will need to be encouraged to become increasingly aware of their own professional development needs as well as the needs of the school. The training, ongoing professional development and deployment of TAs working with children with learning difficulties needs to be considered as part of the school development plan, so that your school has a considerable bank of expertise to call upon, across the board.

TAs should

'...take advantage of planned and incidental self-development opportunities in order to maintain and improve the contribution that they can make to raising pupil achievement. Asking for advice and support to help resolve problems should be seen as a form of strength and professionalism.' (LGNTO, 2001 – p6)

This understanding that it is a professional strength to seek advice and support within one's own institution is the hallmark of a confident and effective TA. Whether it be a simple request about one specific situation, or a greater, overarching concern relating to whole-school issues, the TA should be able to see in-school training and support as having equal validity alongside more formal, external professional development.

'Teaching Assistants are entitled to feel that they can develop in their jobs and get better at what they are doing ... It is also clearly in the interests of the school if its Teaching Assistants are able to increase their expertise and their job satisfaction.' (DfES, 2000 – p34)

Performance management

Supporting the Teaching Assistant sets out a suggested framework for reviewing TAs' performance and promoting their development. Managing this process will include

- undertaking regular appraisal
- revisiting the job description
- assessing the training needs
- providing induction
- using mentors
- examining different forms of training
- undertaking joint training
- encouraging sharing of what is learned
- maintaining a professional development portfolio
- finding finance
- evaluating training.

Undertaking regular appraisal

This is a formal and scheduled opportunity for the TA, together with their line manager, to review and share the celebration of their achievements, discuss their performance, professional needs and any concerns or problems they may have and to look ahead at their career aspirations.

Revisiting the job description

This is a key document in defining what support the TA is expected to provide and it is important that it is kept up to date and that it truly reflects the nature and complexity of the TA's current and developing role.

Assessing the training needs

As the TA gains experience and expertise, she or he will probably want to increase their knowledge and understanding of general or specific aspects of the job. This may be a very specialised study, such as supporting a child with a particular syndrome, or it may be a wider area, such as how children learn. Training opportunities may be accessed through a variety of routes.

Providing induction

This should have started even before the TA took up the post, but may well be a continuing process for a relatively new TA.

The use of mentors

Once the induction process is complete, it will still be useful for each TA to have a mentor within the school, who may be the class teacher with whom they work, a senior TA or even the SEN coordinator. When undertaking NVQ training, the TA will also be assigned to a training mentor or tutor, who may or may not be a member of your staff.

Examining different forms of training

In-school or external, specific or general, practical or award-bearing, there are now as many training routes as there are areas for training in. See Formal qualifications, below.

Undertaking joint training

This is when TAs and those who manage them undertake training together, which helps reinforce teamwork and ensures that both TA and class teacher are thinking along the same lines.

Encouraging sharing of what is learned

Rather than sending all your TAs on a one-day course at great expense and causing short-staffing in the school, provide time for the one TA who attends the course to pass on to his or her colleagues what they learned and how it could be useful in your school. Teachers could join it too, if possible.

A professional development portfolio
Every TA should be encouraged to put together a file including all aspects of their work and their training experience.

Finding finance
Increasing levels of funding are now being made available to schools to provide training opportunities for TAs.

Evaluating training
Reporting on or discussing the value and benefits of training, whether in school or beyond, will be valuable to the trainee in identifying areas of learning and further need and also valuable to the training provider to improve provision for the future.

Appraisal

Appraisal of TAs working with special needs children will probably be your responsibility. As well as being a valuable professional development activity for each individual TA, appraisal will also be a useful opportunity for you as SEN coordinator to identify training needs within and across the team, to determine key skills required and to examine which of the different training routes would be most appropriate to meet these needs. You will then be able to include these identified areas for further training in your team development plan.

A very useful photocopiable blank form entitled 'Framework for an Appraisal' is included in *Supporting the Teaching Assistant*. It is designed specifically for use with TAs.

INSET

Most TAs will appreciate in-school training in areas such as

- supporting aspects of the curriculum, such as literacy, numeracy and ICT
- the school aims and ethos – how their work fits into the whole scheme of things
- behaviour and discipline – the school's policy and practice
- school rules and routines
- confidentiality and people skills
- health and safety issues
- preferred methods of working with teachers and other adults in the school.

To help in the planning of INSET provision for TAs, there is an excellent set of audit materials in *Supporting the Teaching Assistant*, which will help you to identify training needs through evaluating current provision, experience and areas of expertise. Carrying out such an audit will also provide clear guidelines for writing a new action plan for managing and deploying TAs in your school, to ensure optimum provision for the future.

In this book, Chapter 6: Managing INSET considers the different types of support which can be provided in school, both for teachers and for TAs, often together.

> 'Research indicates that some of the most effective training courses for Teaching Assistants are those based in schools as part of the schools' INSET programme.' (DfES, 2000 – p36)

Team meetings

In addition to training and INSET, there will need to be regular meetings for TAs. These may be weekly, monthly or half-termly, according to need, but they must be scheduled well in advance and all TAs must be invited to attend and their overtime funded by the school if they are not normally in school at that time. (This should be budgeted for at the beginning of the year.)

Meetings will not need to be too time-consuming if they are held fairly often. They will be invaluable opportunities for TAs to air and share their concerns, discuss and disseminate aspects of good practice, demonstrate new resources and learn about new initiatives in the field of SEN as well as recent developments and changing demands in the needs of the school. Sometimes these meetings could be for the TAs alone, chaired by the senior TA. More often they will be attended by the headteacher and/or yourself as well as any other relevant personnel.

The successful work of the TAs should be recognised and celebrated to maintain high morale. Any joint gripes or positive points for action should be noted and circulated to all those present as well as members of the senior management team, to be discussed and addressed, in order to improve the service given by the TAs in the school.

Formal qualifications

The government and Local Government National Training Organisation (LGNTO) induction programme for newly appointed TAs is described above. Both this and the NVQs for intermediate and higher level TAs are closely linked to the National Standards.

Level 2 NVQ

The Level 2 NVQ is for TAs who may be recent entrants to the occupation and/or whose work responsibilities are limited in scope. Level 2 could lead on into Level 3 when the TA is ready to take this step, at which point they will be able to take forward credits from Level 2 as part of the Level 3 qualification.

Level 2 is made up of four mandatory units, plus the choice of three further units from a list of five options, which includes four of the Level 3 units. The mandatory units for Level 2 are

2.1 Help with classroom resources and records

2.2 Help with the care and support of pupils

2.3 Provide support for learning activities

2.4 Provide effective support for your colleagues.

Level 3 NVQ

The Level 3 NVQ is designed for experienced TAs, whose working roles call for competence across a variety of responsibilities. At Level 3, TAs will be required to achieve four mandatory units, plus six chosen units, from a selection of 19 choices, ranging across pupil, teacher, school and curriculum support. The mandatory units at this level are

3.1 Contribute to the management of pupil behaviour

3.2 Establish and maintain relationships with individual pupils and groups

3.3 Support pupils during learning activities

3.4 Review and develop your own professional practice.

Other qualifications

Before the induction programme and NVQs were introduced, the only formal training qualifications for TAs were

- STA (Specialist Teaching Assistant) course, usually based at a college and requiring weekly attendance and further study over a year or more
- BTEC, also school or college-based
- City and Guilds Certificate in Learning Support, again usually college-based
- NNEB, or variations of this, which focus on early years support and are therefore not appropriate to most SEN TAs.

Deployment of teaching assistants

'Schools report greater job effectiveness and greater job satisfaction where the management of TAs is active (without being intrusive), rather than TAs just being "left to get on with it" in class.' (DfES, 2000 – p20)

The first and most important factor is that TAs should always be given specific, purposeful tasks, with clear objectives and access to appropriate resources. They need to be able to plan and discuss activities and their outcomes with the teacher or other adults involved. They need to be able to input to assessment and target-setting for the children they support and they need sufficient time for preparation, clearing up and record-keeping. They need to know they are doing a good job and they need to feel valued.

Creating a partnership with the teacher

A good partnership between teacher and TA will depend upon their respective responsibilities being clearly defined and understood by both parties and on the mutual respect and trust which they build up, enabling both of them to fulfil their roles effectively.

Communication

Open channels of communication are crucial to the effectiveness of the TA, whatever their role. This obviously includes opportunities for joint planning, discussion and reflection, but time is at such a premium in a busy school day that we need to be creative in the ways we find to communicate. In addition to a few minutes before and after the school day, some class teachers evolve a system with their TAs which enables two-way communication on an ongoing basis.

The 'day-to-day' box

This might take the form of a box in which to place lesson plans, timetables, notes, news, differentiated worksheets, SEN activities, observation and record sheets, etc. There might also, or instead, be an exercise book or loose-leaf file in which the TA can keep plans, notes and records and through which they can let each other know on a daily basis what is going on and how children are responding.

The 'to do' box

This is a magazine file box in which anyone (headteacher, teachers, SEN coordinator, administration officer, chair of governors or chair of PTA) can place anything they want photocopied, bound, laminated, stapled, distributed, etc. Mark them as 'anytime' or 'urgent' and TAs do them in any of the brief time-slots they might find between activities, during the day. It may be that your school has assigned one particular TA to undertake these tasks, or to be attached to particular people so that, for example, you always give your photocopying to the same person to do for you. If this is the case, it will be helpful if it is someone already familiar with SEN documents and resources.

Resources

TAs need to have ready access to all the learning support resources they will need to support children effectively in the classroom. However, they will also need some general stationery and other resources for their own use. Too often, schools make sure that teachers and the administration officer have all these things, but forget to provide them for others in the school.

Planning

'...all the evidence shows that the team of teacher and TA works at its highest level when the TA is informed by the teacher of the plans and intentions for the lesson and is consulted over their execution.' (DfES, 2000 – p24)

A TA needs to have an input into lesson planning, or at least a sight of lesson plans a day or more before the lesson. They may need to adapt activities to be accessible for an individual statemented child or for a learning difficulties group. Most SEN children need to use additional practical apparatus to help them understand or practise new skills and concepts and the TA will need to ensure that they have all the appropriate resources in the classroom, ready to use. They will also, crucially, need to know what the learning objectives and the desired outcomes are so that they can assess the progress and attainment of their children and can steer them in the right direction or reinforce the key points. Without all this preparation, the TA will not be in a position to ensure optimum learning.

Added to this, the TA attached to a particular child or group will know from experience certain details, such as the maximum concentration span, the rate of writing or the extent of distance-vision of those children, which the teacher may need to bear in mind as part of the planning process. They will also be able to build into the planning the way the children responded in the last lesson on this topic and what this might suggest to enhance their learning in the next.

The planning sheet on page 86 provides a user-friendly framework for the TA to use in preparing for each lesson. They should be able to fill this in from the teacher's plans, or better still fill it in with the teacher. It helps if the teacher's lesson planning, usually done on a weekly basis, is available ahead of the first day, so that, for example, the plan for Monday to Friday is available on the previous Friday. If this is difficult because the teacher only completes their planning at the weekend, perhaps they could try planning Tuesday to Monday, so that the TA already has plans for Monday's lessons from the previous week.

Five things TAs need to know to support learning

A TA needs a full understanding of what is planned in a lesson in order to work effectively.

1 The learning objective – the purpose of the activity.
2 The activity – what you will be doing and what resources they will need.
3 The outcome – the result of the activity, ie. the finished work.
4 How long? – duration of the activity or required support.
5 Who is it for? – which children.

Target-setting, reviewing and record-keeping

SEN TAs should always participate in setting targets (for example in IEPs) and reviewing the progress of the children with whom they work, for they know best what the children can and can't do, what they might be able to work towards and what support might be needed along the way.

To help TAs to contribute effectively to this process, you might like to make use of some kind of agreed observation and assessment recording sheet format. Consider using one of the photocopiable observation sheets at the end of this chapter. The first is designed for use with a group of up to six children. The other is for more detailed use with one SEN child. Alternatively, design your own, perhaps tailor-made to the individual children.

Whatever format you choose to use, it will be useful if these records, when used with SEN children, are kept together in a folder for each child, so that they can readily be consulted and so that progress (or otherwise) is immediately noticeable.

TAs as reading mentors

As well as all the planned tasks, there are always a number of other child-centred activities that need doing, such as hearing children read, or helping them to organise or mount their work.

In some schools, TAs are assigned to a particular class or to specific children as reading mentors. In this way they can support the reading of children whose reading development is delayed, on a daily or at least a regular basis.

The advantage of this is that the child gets used to reading to a particular adult and thus the progress can be built on day by day and celebrated together.

It also gives the child an opportunity to build up a one-to-one relationship with an adult in the school, which can often be helpful in supporting the child's emotional well-being as well as encouraging them to achieve their potential.

Case studies of good practice

Further ideas regarding approaches to the deployment of TAs and creative use of their time in support of the school, the teacher, the children and the curriculum, can be found on the Teachernet website (www.teachernet.gov.uk). Search for 'teaching assistants' to find a number of very good case studies of good practice.

The way forward

The DfES consultation document *Developing the Role of School Support Staff* explains the government's plans for increasing and developing the TA workforce. According to the document, the government will

> '...clarify the circumstances under which support staff can undertake "teaching activities" ... some teaching activity can be undertaken by suitably trained staff without Qualified Teacher Status, provided they are working within a system of leadership and supervision provided by the qualified teacher. Determining what should be delegated, and the nature and extent of supervision, should primarily be a matter for the professional judgement of headteachers and qualified teachers rather than for rigid national demarcation.' (2002, Executive summary)

In terms of developing the training and development of TAs, the government proposes to encourage the development of three broad routes of career progression, which are

1 pedagogical

2 behaviour and guidance

3 administration and organisation.

There will be further training materials developed for both TAs and the teachers with whom they work. Additional Advanced Skills Teachers with particular skills and experience in working with and managing support staff will be appointed. The National College for School Leadership will work with the DfES and others to develop training programmes for school leaders to support all the new developments. A new framework for the teacher–support staff relationship will be produced. Additional funding will be made available.

References

Centre for Educational Needs, University of Manchester (1999) *The Management, Role and Training of Learning Support Assistants*. London: DfES.

DfES (2000) *Supporting the Teaching Assistant: A Good Practice Guide*. Ref: 148/2000. London: DfES.

DfES (2001) *Special Educational Needs Code of Practice*. Ref: 581/2001. London: DfES.

LGNTO (2001) *National Occupational Standards for Teaching/Classroom Assistants*. London: LGNTO.

Ofsted (2002) *Teaching Assistants in Primary Schools: An Evaluation by Ofsted 2001–2002*. London: Ofsted.

DfES (2002) *Developing the Role of School Support Staff*. London: DfES.

Thanks to Fiona Gibson, Robin Hammerton and Graham Reeves for their contributions to this chapter.

Lesson planning sheet

1 The learning objective (The purpose of the activity)

2 The activity (What you will be doing and what resources you need)

3 The outcome (The result of the activity – the finished work)

4 How long? (duration of activity/support)

5 Who is it for? (Which child/ren)

Notes and reminders

Group observation and recording sheet

Date _____ **Class** _____

Year group _____ **Teacher** _____

Lesson/activity

Lesson objective

Key vocabulary

Children's names	Assessment	Observation notes and comments

Assessment Key
✓ = fully understood
○ = partially understood, but needs some consolidation
✗ = not understood (or very little understood)

Additional comments (behaviour, attitudes, etc.)

Individual observation and recording sheet

Name   **Date**

Class   **Year group**   **Teacher**

Lesson/activity

Lesson objective

Key vocabulary

Learning

Attitude/behaviour

General comments

Child's self-assessment (to be filled in by child)

	☺	😐	☹
Learning			
Behaviour			
	very good	**so-so**	**not so good**

CHAPTER 6
Managing INSET

One of the principal themes in the 1997 green paper *Excellence for All Children* was the boosting of opportunities for staff development in SEN and the dissemination of good practice. This was further underpinned in the 2001 SEN Code of Practice, which stated that one of the key responsibilities of SEN coordinators is 'contributing to the in-service training of staff' (DfES, 2001 – 5:32). Not only does this require your active participation in leading INSET in school, but the Code of Practice also makes clear that you have a key role to play in ensuring that teachers are fully involved in the identification, assessment and monitoring of SEN children's needs.

This means that teachers need to be kept up to date with SEN developments in and beyond the school, and to be given appropriate support and training to enable them to fulfil their role effectively. You will want not only to support class teachers, but also to show them that they all have valuable contributions to make and much to learn from a concerted whole-school approach towards meeting the needs of all children.

Identifying teachers' training and support needs

Generally speaking, teachers will have identified their own specific needs regarding SEN through self-review and appraisal as part of the performance management process. New situations, and particularly new children coming into their classes, may make additional demands on them and these also need to be addressed. Teachers may need to understand more about some of the problems and conditions of SEN children, as well as strategies for balancing the needs of these children with the teaching of the class as a whole and making optimum use of any available support staff.

As SEN coordinator, you will have further opportunities, both formally and informally through the course of your work, to identify teachers' professional development needs.

These opportunities will include

- informal liaison with teachers regarding specific challenges and how to deal with them
- ongoing informal liaison with teachers regarding general everyday difficulties encountered
- trouble-shooting, particularly when a new child arrives and initial needs have to be identified quickly (eg. ADHD or Autistic Spectrum Disorders)
- discussions about individual teachers' interests (academic or practical) in exploring unfamiliar areas of SEN
- individual teachers' agreed performance management targets as communicated to you by the head or team leader
- introduction and implementation of whole-school initiatives and policy developments
- whole-school SEN audit or self-review.

Relating needs to the school improvement plan

Most schools' development or improvement plans will include aspects identified as priorities within the LEA's education plan, as well as specific areas of focus identified within their own SEN action plan. School improvement plans are usually also based on reviews or audits carried out by the whole staff or at least by the senior management team, and will thus be likely to include whole-school needs, as well as the requirements of groups of staff, both teaching and support staff. It is worth noting here that the training, ongoing professional development and deployment of teaching assistants working with children with learning difficulties needs to be considered as part of the school improvement plan, so that your school has a considerable bank of expertise to call upon.

Less likely to be included in the whole-school development or improvement plan will be the needs or aspirations of individual teachers. However, these may be identified in the ways outlined above.

In prioritising needs and planning professional development to meet these needs, decisions will have been taken about the cost and resource implications. External courses or support need to be included in the costings. However, wherever possible, in-school training will be comparatively inexpensive, more responsive to specific need and easier to arrange. This obviously has considerable implications for you as SEN coordinator. There may be times when a mixture of these two approaches might be desirable, or perhaps you could invite other local schools to join you in funding the services of an external specialist trainer.

A whole-school approach

While professional development and support may often be delivered on an individual or group basis, it is crucial that you as SEN coordinator are able to see the whole picture and to orchestrate an ongoing whole-school approach. However, this will need to be a shared responsibility.

'...a SENCO cannot do everything single-handedly. It is the responsibility of all teachers and support staff in a school

- to be aware of the school's responsibilities for children with special educational needs
- to have regard to the guidance in the Code of Practice
- to apply that guidance effectively in assessing and teaching children with SEN
- to work together in the classroom to raise standards for all pupils.' (DfEE, 1997)

Professional development visits

In addition to school-based and external INSET and support, it will often be very helpful to build in opportunities for teachers and teaching assistants to visit resource centres to explore the range of materials available or to schools that are centres of good practice to observe approaches to working with SEN children. Similarly, arranging a visit to an SEN unit attached to a mainstream school may be very helpful in observing the behaviours and responses of children with specific conditions and for learning new strategies for dealing with and integrating such children in mainstream classrooms. In certain cases, such as children with Down syndrome and some physical disabilities, teachers will find it useful to liaise with and visit resource centres and special schools to seek advice regarding special resources and equipment. Outreach may well be available and funded.

An SEN library

A useful way of providing informal support to colleagues is by setting up an SEN library and information centre. This may be just a corner in the staffroom, or it could be a small room in the school if available.

An SEN library and information centre could contain

- guidance on the Code of Practice
- leaflets relating to specific SEN conditions
- SEN magazines and articles
- reference books on specific SEN conditions
- the school SEN policy
- copies of LEA reviews
- copies of IEPs
- a copy of the SEN register, if the school still keeps a register
- information on local and national support groups
- useful website listings
- resource catalogues
- information for parents
- positive messages about SEN in the school.

School-based INSET

While SEN coordinators are often expected to be the resident experts on a wide range of special educational needs, not every SEN coordinator feels confident in leading formal INSET sessions, particularly in areas of special needs in which they may feel that they lack expertise. In such cases it may be more effective to organise and coordinate INSET sessions that are delivered by other professionals. Such sessions can be extremely productive, especially when shared with other schools in the area, or with schools of a similar type.

However, you will want to deliver more informal INSET training to your colleagues in areas of expertise and common concern. Such training may take the form of staff meetings (or regular staff meeting SEN bulletins), whole or part INSET days or in-class INSET, which focus on modelling and sharing skills.

In planning school-based INSET, consider the contributions that can be made by other members of teaching or support staff who may have gained experience of working with children who have specific types of special educational needs, such as autistic spectrum disorders.

It is important that you keep your teacher and teaching assistant colleagues up to date on SEN procedures within the school, particularly those relating to

- roles and responsibilities detailed in the Code of Practice
- LEA review procedures
- school SEN monitoring and assessment procedures.

It is also helpful to operate an 'open door' policy, which encourages colleagues to feel that they can talk to you informally about specific problems. This initial chat may well highlight an area of difficulty that is common to a number of staff within the school and you might find it useful to organise a group INSET or question and answer session, with the aim of offering practical help and advice. Such a planned session is often more helpful than trying to offer quick fixes via a hasty break-time discussion in the staffroom. It may also be more useful than trying to deliver whole-school INSET on issues that do not affect or concern all members of the teaching staff.

School-based development for teaching assistants

Good working relationships between teachers and teaching assistants, an awareness of team needs, and recognition that SEN issues are part of whole-school development should form the background to effective professional development for teaching assistants.

Some of the most useful, practical training takes place in school on an ongoing basis, such as

- observing what happens in the classroom with colleagues
- learning from other teaching assistants
- developing and using different strategies for coping with a variety of situations and different children's needs.

However it is important that teaching assistants should also experience more formal training in order to develop the skills and expertise required for both team and individual development. There are a number of external and professional training options now open to teaching assistants. The following is a brief overview of what is available. See Chapter 5: Teaching assistants for more information.

Formal training for teaching assistants can be delivered through

- a school-based SEN INSET programme for teaching assistants
- a school-based SEN INSET programme for teachers and teaching assistants together
- a school-based curriculum INSET programme for TAs (such as reading development or supporting children in the numeracy hour)
- specialist training courses delivered by professionals in school or elsewhere
- LEA training courses (accredited and non-accredited) such as NVQ qualifications
- higher education accredited courses.

As SEN coordinator, you will be responsible for devising a programme of training designed to cover some of the key skills required for teaching assistants working with children with learning difficulties in your school. This will be particularly appropriate for newly appointed teaching assistants or for those not undertaking NVQ accreditation. Even for experienced colleagues, such INSET will be an opportunity to agree methods of working, to understand the school's own policy requirements and to ensure continuity in your particular school. Areas which you may need to cover, depending on the experience of your teaching assistants, could include

- responses to behaviour difficulties
- building children's self-esteem
- making and modifying curriculum materials
- knowledge of the SEN Code of Practice
- working with IEPs
- using specialist equipment and techniques (such as lifting a disabled child)
- using ICT across the curriculum
- working with planning documents
- making observations and keeping informal records
- contributing to children's reviews.

It is part of your role as SEN coordinator to be aware of the training needs of your team and to include these in your team development plan. Training together can reinforce teamwork and improve skills for teachers and teaching assistants. It is important to make sure that appropriate finances are available and their use well planned. The government has allocated funds specifically for the deployment and professional development of teaching assistants, so this should promote a positive outlook.

Leading INSET sessions

Although the greater part of your work involves informal and ongoing support, there will be areas of special educational needs within the school that require a slightly more formal INSET session. Such sessions are often incorporated into planned after-school meeting times and reflect the needs identified through the school improvement or development plan and the SEN action plan.

If you are asked to lead an INSET session, it is important to remember that your audience is made up of classroom teachers who are often coping with a wide range of needs within a large, mixed-ability class.

Whole-school SEN INSET

When leading whole-school SEN INSET, deliver the following messages.

☐ SEN issues are regarded as a shared whole-school responsibility.

☐ You, as SEN coordinator, are just one of the staff (albeit the leader and major contributor) responsible for developing strategies to support children with learning difficulties.

☐ You are sharing your experience and knowledge, rather than trying to be an expert in a specific area.

Make sure that

☐ background information about specific SEN issues is relevant to children in the school, not just based on academic research

☐ you present the information using accessible and teacher-friendly language, avoiding acronyms and jargon as far as possible

☐ any strategies suggested for inclusion can realistically be managed within a mixed-ability class

☐ activities suggested for support are practical and incorporate a range of ideas for differentiation (eg. pictorial representation, mind-maps, stepped tasks, etc.).

Leading an INSET session provides you with an opportunity to share your own interest and enthusiasm for special educational needs with all members of staff. It also opens up valuable channels of communication with regard to general SEN issues, which you may want to follow up in more detail at a future date. Such issues might include

- differentiation
- classroom-based assessment and monitoring

- strategies to support SEN children during literacy and numeracy hours
- behavioural support
- the raising of self-esteem
- working effectively with teaching assistants
- ICT as a tool for learning for SEN children
- working with parents and outside agencies
- developing and implementing IEPs
- record-keeping and report-writing.

Blueprint for a successful INSET session

The advantages in your leading SEN INSET in your school (rather than an outside specialist) include the following.

- You know the school, the children and the staff in a way that no external INSET provider can ever do.
- Being employed by the school as SEN coordinator, you won't cost extra in terms of fees or supply cover.
- You will have attended specialist courses and will be able to pass on what you have learned yourself.
- INSET provided to the whole staff means that teachers and teaching assistants get a consistent, controlled input that can't be guaranteed when they go individually to courses elsewhere.
- Undertaking INSET together within the school provides an opportunity to follow up the session through informal discussions and investigation.
- Having the whole staff together for school-based INSET gives you the opportunity to deliver clear and specific messages to them all at once and without suggesting that anyone in particular is the recipient of the message.

However, the responsibility of leading school-based INSET is often not relished by SEN coordinators. Being regarded as the resident expert in your area (and expected to know about a vast and ever-increasing range of SEN topics), you are required to pass on your expertise to others. In addition to teachers and teaching assistants, these others may include governors, midday supervisors, volunteer helpers and groups of interested parents. Misgivings about the process shared by many SEN coordinators include the following.

- You might feel that your strengths lie in teaching and working with SEN children or supporting colleagues on an informal basis, rather than 'lecturing' to adults

- You might feel nervous about facing a group of people you know well. For some people this can be more daunting than facing a roomful of strangers.

- You may find it difficult to think of user-friendly ways to effectively pass on the essence of what you have learned elsewhere and in greater depth.

- You are almost certainly very busy and may find it very difficult to find the time to prepare as fully as you would like.

The success of any INSET session will depend on the thinking and care you take over planning your preparation, presentation and evaluation. The following suggestions should help you to overcome at least some of your misgivings and make an INSET session more helpful. Even if you have no qualms about putting yourself in front of a group of colleagues and have a fund of attention-grabbing and imaginative ways of communication and of involving and motivating others, these suggestions will help you increase the effectiveness of your sessions.

Preparation

Just as it is crucial to be specific about learning objectives when planning a lesson, so it is crucial to be clear when planning an INSET session about what you intend the learning outcomes to be. Unless you are absolutely certain about what the INSET is designed to achieve, it is unlikely that it will achieve very much at all. The foremost intention of any INSET, of course, will be to improve the quality of education you provide for the children. But, how do you intend to do this?

The first area for consideration is the theme. This may already have been identified, but you will still need to plan your focus and the angle you want to take. This will lead you into setting your objectives. From the beginning, everyone will need to know the purpose of the session. You will clarify this if you start the session by saying something like 'By the end of this session... .'

Next, you will have to decide about the presenter. Usually, this will be you, the expert in the school on all SEN matters. You know the subject and you know the context of the school, its organisation, resources and personnel.

However, you might also want to involve other people within the school. Perhaps a teacher or teaching assistant has done some particularly successful work with children in an aspect of SEN that

you want to focus on, or perhaps a member of staff has attended an external course on a particularly relevant topic. Alternatively, you might want to work alongside or hand over to someone from another school, or a peripatetic learning support teacher or other professional.

If anyone else is going to join you, make sure you have briefed them fully about their role in the session, the timing of their contribution and what is expected of them.

You will need to think about timing – how much time you will need and at what point in the school day. This may already have been agreed between you and the headteacher. However, it will be helpful to consider the implications of this timing for your audience.

Similarly, you may not have a choice of venue, but if you have you will want to consider where would be most appropriate for what you want to do. The staffroom may be the obvious choice, but sometimes the hall or the library or a classroom might be more suitable for some types of INSET.

When you have decided where the session will take place, you will need to consider the layout of the room. This can influence the effectiveness of your INSET.

Seating

Comfortable chairs might be informal and put everyone at ease, but they won't necessarily encourage full attention.

Layout

- A **boardroom** layout involves everyone sitting around a large table, which helps to focus things and creates a business-like atmosphere, although this might not be appropriate for practical activities or small-group discussion.

- A **theatre** layout is when everyone faces the front, which can be good for presentations, particularly if people have to look at a screen or flipchart, but it doesn't necessarily encourage active participation.

- A **lounge** layout is the more usual staff-room situation, which makes everyone feel more relaxed and is useful for informal and small-group discussions, but less likely to promote a business-like atmosphere or to encourage optimum concentration.

- A **classroom** layout is just that. It is the most appropriate for practical INSET sessions, such as workshops, but may be uncomfortable for adults over an extended period of time.

Finally, once you have done all the planning and informed staff where and when the INSET will take place, make sure they know what the focus of the session will be and whether they need to prepare for it in any way or bring anything in particular along.

Presentation

Choosing a format is the next task. This will usually be one or a combination of

- talk
- discussion
- demonstration
- workshop.

The most meticulous preparation in the world is of little use if the presentation is wrong. The best format will largely depend on what you want to achieve and the nature of the subject matter.

Each format has its own advantages and is suited to particular purposes. A talk, illustrated with overhead transparencies or using PowerPoint, is a good way to communicate information. Discussion allows people to express their views and to come to a decision. A demonstration provides a visual instruction in a specific technique (such as how to lift a disabled child or the optimum seating position for handwriting). A workshop can encourage the learning and development of a range of skills. Most INSET sessions will need to include a combination of at least two of these formats. You will find it helpful to decide on the timings for each section of the INSET session.

Using equipment to illustrate your presentation

Equipment (such as a computer, a projector or a flipchart) can be useful, as long as it is used as a tool to achieve a set purpose. It should not dictate what you do or be a crutch to rely on. If you do decide to use equipment to help you with your presentation, the following points may help.

- Everyone in your audience should have a clear line of view (try not to put yourself between your audience and the screen).
- Materials should be selected carefully (eg. don't show a whole video when just a part of it is really relevant).
- Overhead transparencies are best in a fairly large and clear font (such as Arial at 18 point) and a border round the edge makes them look more professional.
- Computerised presentations can be very effective, but not at too fast a pace or with too many changes.

- Whether using overhead transparencies or a computer, conciseness is the key. Four or five bullet points are much more effective than the whole page crammed full of text.
- Handouts are valuable as they avoid the need for your audience to take copious notes and they ensure that everyone has all the details of what was said. However, do go through them all, at least briefly, during the session, as busy teachers will rarely be able to find the time to read through lengthy handouts in full after the event.

Awkward silences

While discussion can be an effective format for part of an INSET session, it can result in uncomfortable silences. Awkward silences can be avoided by

- giving clear questions around which discussion can take place
- setting a time limit for each discussion
- acknowledging or praising contributions, to encourage more.

Dominant participants

The other problem with discussions can be that one participant talks too much, taking over the situation and discouraging involvement from all the others, or diverting the discussion away from the main focus. Over-dominant talkers can be discouraged by

- taking back control by reminding your colleagues about the intended outcomes
- bringing the discussion back on course through your own intervention
- identifying a later time when a different issue can be aired.

Action and evaluation

Don't let the INSET session drift to an end – use the final minutes to summarise the main points of the session and to decide what will happen next. Ideally, any INSET session should end with some sort of agreed action plan, such as 'Following this INSET, we will...'. The outcomes of the session, including any agreed action plan, should be recorded in the form of a statement, notes or brief minutes. Then this action plan can be followed up and reviewed over time (after a month, then after a term), assessing to what extent and how successfully the plan was implemented.

Your evaluation should focus on the objectives you originally set. To a large extent, these will have been expressed in terms of the effect on teaching and learning. Therefore, the success or otherwise of the

Techniques for developing speaking skills

For many people, speaking in public is not an easy task. However, the good news is that there are some well-tried techniques which may help you to develop these skills.

Prepare

- Make sure you prepare your script well and write it out in detail to begin with.

Make notes

- Make notes of the main points of your script, perhaps on one sheet of A4 paper, or on postcard-sized cards. You may find it useful to use a highlighter for the key words and phrases to help you find them if you are feeling flustered.

Rehearse

- Rehearse your presentation. Read out the whole script at first, word for word if necessary. Do this a few times if you feel you need to. This will help you to learn the flow of the content, which will help you to gain confidence in what you are going to say.

  Then try rehearsing it, using just the cards, looking up as much as possible. It will be useful to rehearse the introduction at least in front of a trusted colleague or friend if you can arrange it, so that you can benefit from some constructive feedback and some further confidence boosting.

Repeat key points

- Repeating the key points is usually a useful technique. (Sustained listening is more difficult than reading or speaking and it is natural for listeners to miss some snatches of information.)

Use relaxation techniques

- Relaxation techniques, such as deep breathing and keeping the shoulders down will enable you to speak more naturally.

Remove distractions

- Remove all distractions, such as keys or coins in your pocket or anything you might feel tempted to fidget with.

Move around

- Try to move around a little (but not too much!) Being rooted rigidly to one spot can be as distracting for your listeners as too much bobbing about.

Make eye-contact

- Make frequent eye-contact with individuals around the room. This will have the joint effect of making what you say seem more personal and relevant to your audience and of seeing and making use of immediate responses, such as nods for agreement or shakes of the head in disagreement.

Smile

- Smile when you speak (but try not to grin inanely!). Your smiles will emphasise the positive messages you want to give and encourage your audience to listen more attentively.

Speak slowly

- Slow down your speech (but not too much so that it becomes completely unnatural). Leave pauses between key points so that they have a chance to sink in, but try not to make your pauses so long that you give the impression of having forgotten what you want to say next.

Be occasionally light-hearted

- It is often a useful ploy to throw in something light-hearted every now and then, if you can. In the school context, this could be a child's quote, or a brief anecdote involving children.

MANAGING INSET

INSET should be judged by the degree to which the children's education has been improved.

A questionnaire or follow-up discussion which asks about content, delivery, resources and so on will provide useful information. Try to discover the following information.

1 Do colleagues feel that the session met the stated objectives?

2 Has their knowledge increased?

3 Do they have a better understanding?

4 Have their skills been developed?

5 Has the INSET affected the way they are likely to teach or support children in the future?

Alternatively, or additionally, evaluation can be through classroom observations. This will help in a very direct way to evaluate whether and how appropriate changes have been implemented.

Success criteria

As an effective SEN coordinator, you will be able to see the successful outcomes of your input into the professional development of your colleagues in a number of ways.

You will see children who

• are learning happily alongside their own peer group

• have confidence in themselves as learners

• have made progress towards targets set in their IEPs

• have developed self-esteem within the school community.

You will also work alongside colleagues who

• are able to recognise children with specific learning difficulties

• know how and where to access SEN information and support

• understand their role and responsibilities within the Code of Practice

• share the writing and monitoring of IEPs

• identify their own SEN professional development needs

• feel confident about their role in supporting children with special educational needs.

Evaluating the outcomes of your input into the professional development of your colleagues can often be quite subjective if undertaken by you alone. It is therefore useful to ask your headteacher or SEN governor to take a more objective view and to report back to you. In this way you can develop an ongoing dialogue and a clearer perspective, not just on positive outcomes for teachers, children and for the whole school, but also on opportunities for following up and extending professional development opportunities for all staff in the future.

Finally

Organising INSET is one of the ways in which you, as SEN coordinator, can make a difference to what happens in all parts of your school. You can have a positive influence on the practice of your colleagues and, through them, on the attainment, achievements and well-being of the children. By following the advice in this chapter, you can make sure that the positive effect you have is both far-reaching and long-lasting for the benefit of everyone in your school.

References

DfEE (1997) *Excellence for all Children*. London: TSO.

DfES (2001) *SEN Code of Practice*. Ref: 581/2001. London: DfES.

Thanks to Graham Reeves for his contributions to this chapter.

CHAPTER 7

Working with parents

Working with parents is an important part of your role for some obvious reasons. Not only do you and your colleagues have a responsibility to be in contact with parents, but parents also need to know who to come to with their concerns and anxieties. But the importance of this aspect of your role goes further than that. We know that developing partnerships with parents has great benefits for the children in our care.

> 'Partnership with parents plays a key role in promoting a culture of co-operation between parents, schools, LEAs and others. This is important in enabling children and young people with SEN to achieve their potential.'
> (DfES, 2001 – 2:1)

The school is usually the first and main point of contact for parents. Schools **must** tell parents when they first identify that a child has special educational needs. Parents' participation in all stages of the SEN process, developing and implementing a joint learning approach, should be encouraged and welcomed.

The 2001 SEN Code of Practice devotes a whole chapter to working with parents and the importance of this partnership is echoed throughout the document. It makes it clear that this partnership is an equal one.

> 'Parents hold key information and have a critical role to play in their children's education. They have unique strengths, knowledge and experience to contribute to the shared view of a child's needs and the best ways of supporting them. It is therefore essential that all professionals actively seek to work with parents and value the contribution they make.' (DfES, 2001 – 2:2)

Parents should be supported and empowered to

- realise their responsibilities as parents
- play an active part in their children's education
- know and understand what their SEN children are entitled to
- express their views and concerns
- be able to access appropriate information, advice and support.

Parental responsibility

As SEN coordinator, you will need to clarify who has parental responsibility for any SEN children. Usually, this will be jointly shared by the parents of the child. However, if the parents are not living together or if there is a single parent, this responsibility may rest solely with the parent with whom the child is residing. If the child is living with other adults (such as grandparents) they will probably have this responsibility on a day-to-day basis. Finally, if the child is in a foster home or in care, you will need to ascertain who is the first point of contact on any matters relating to their education and well-being. Throughout this chapter, the word 'parents' is used to describe the role of parents or carers.

Key principles

Positive attitudes and access to user-friendly information are essential features to successful parent partnership. Such a partnership will be based on mutual respect, in which all parties understand that working together will facilitate optimum progress for SEN children.

Key principles require education professionals to

- acknowledge and value parents' special knowledge and expertise regarding their child
- focus on each child's strengths in identifying and addressing their needs
- empathise with parents' concerns, difficulties and feelings
- ensure that parents are helped to understand and be prepared as fully as possible before discussions and meetings
- recognise that there may be differing but equally valid points of view involved
- respect and support parents' own needs in coming to terms with and addressing their children's difficulties
- respect parents' wishes as paramount, even if these seem to conflict with what the school perceives to be the best interests of the child.

Parents in the SEN policy

Every school must have an SEN policy document, which should reflect the rights of parents and should enshrine the principles of partnership. Some schools will choose to write a separate policy for parental participation. Either way, it is important for you, as SEN coordinator, to reread all your school's policies closely and critically, from the point of view of parents' involvement in the identification, assessment, provision for and monitoring of their children's needs. You may well need to discuss this with the headteacher, the senior management team, the SEN governor and indeed all teachers and teaching assistants.

The school may need to rewrite some policies and you may need to do some work to raise awareness for all teaching and support staff. As part of this process, it will be useful to focus together, during staff meetings perhaps, on the range of skills and approaches needed to enhance parents' participation in their children's education.

The SEN policy should be written in language that is accessible to parents, who should be given a copy to read if they wish. The policy should cover such things as

- how parents can make their concerns known
- how to let parents know about your concerns
- involving parents in identifying targets for IEPs
- consulting and informing parents about provision
- informing parents and eliciting their impressions of attainments and progress
- encouraging parents to help both at home and at school
- involving parents in reviews and other meetings
- helping parents to understand procedures and supporting them in making contributions
- apprising parents of services outside school such as voluntary agencies and support groups
- informing parents about what they can do if they are dissatisfied.

There needs to be a clear process for parents to make complaints and for the school to address and hopefully resolve such matters. This needs to be set out in the SEN policy and all parents should be encouraged to follow the stated procedure. However, if you make sure that parents are fully informed, supported and involved at all stages, it should be possible to consider and take into account any concerns they might have as soon as they arise and thereby avoid the need to make use of the procedure.

Two-way communications

'These partnerships can be challenging, requiring positive attitudes by all, and in some circumstances additional support and encouragement for parents.' (DfES, 2001 – 2:3)

The starting point for involving parents is good communication. You need a situation in which

- parents feel able to approach the school about any concerns
- parents are receptive to what teachers say
- teachers are responsive to what parents say.

Do the parents at your school know who to approach if they want to discuss their child's progress or difficulties? This may seem obvious to everyone who works in the school, but parents of children with special educational needs are often uncertain. Consider whether your school's policy is clear and whether it has been communicated effectively to parents.

- Should parents approach the class teacher or the headteacher?
- Should they perhaps approach the SEN governor?
- Do they know that the school has an SEN governor and who it is?
- Should they speak to you, as SEN coordinator?
- Do they know that you are the SEN coordinator and, if so, do they know what that means and what you do?

If parents don't know who to approach, it's possible that they will approach no one and, at best, this will delay the resolution of any problems. At worst, problems will escalate and this might lead to confrontations and disputes.

Similarly, class teachers may not be aware of how and whether to contact parents if they think there might be a difficulty.

- Does the class teacher wait until the next parents' meeting to talk to parents (who might not even come)?
- Do they send a letter to explain their concerns?
- Do they invite parents to make an appointment to visit the school?
- Do they tell you so that you can contact the parents?

- Do they tell the headteacher and leave it to her or him to deal with?

- Should they speak to the SEN governor about it?

It's a good idea to have in place an agreed procedure for this process, which should be set out clearly in the policy as well as discussed with any new members of staff.

As one of the main sources of support for parents and usually the first point of contact, class teachers have to be skilled at talking to parents about their child's progress and listening and responding to their concerns. Parents will want to feel confident about approaching teachers when they want support, answers to questions or problems resolved. They will want to discuss a wide range of issues concerning their children's education and they will have many questions, which might include the following.

- What difficulties does my child face?

- How will my child get the help he or she needs?

- How will this help be organised?

- What can I do to help my child at home?

- Is there anybody else who can help?

- How does my child compare with other children in the class?

- What if I disagree with any decisions the school makes?

Good communication doesn't happen naturally. Nor is it something you can suddenly put into place when a child has, or might have, special educational needs. Effective communication skills have to be developed over time and across everything the school does. As SEN coordinator, you may well be the best person to provide appropriate training for teachers, and possibly teaching assistants, in communication skills.

Speaking to parents

The most important factors for class teachers talking to parents are to

- be open and honest with parents, but do it sensitively

- listen attentively and respond sympathetically, whatever their concerns

- speak in plain English – try to avoid jargon

- try to adopt an approach which is optimistic and encouraging

- balance the negative with the positive – praise the child's strengths.

Involving parents informally

It is possible to involve parents informally through

- impromptu conversations and discussions at the beginning or end of the school day

- a home–school contact book of some kind, often linked to the child's reading

- parents working or helping in the school.

Impromptu conversations can work very well for those children whose parents accompany them to and from school each day. They give you or the class teacher valuable opportunities to pass on information to parents quickly and effectively, to share news concerning the child, either at school or at home, and to develop a positive rapport with each other.

If children travel by bus or are accompanied by child-minders, it may be better to keep the channels of communication open on a day-to-day basis through the home–school book, which can be used in a similar way to the impromptu meetings described above. It is important to bear in mind that there will almost certainly be a few parents who either cannot read or who have difficulty in reading and may have to ask someone else, often one of their own children, to read your messages to them. This is a sensitive issue. Remember to be discreet if you think this may be the case.

Another method of informal communication is opened up if parents are working or helping in the school. Whether they are midday supervisors, Teaching assistants or voluntary classroom helpers, parents who are often in school and who are familiar with school routines and procedures are more comfortable with the staff and feel more at home in the school. They will often find it easier to mention concerns and discuss any matters relating to provision for their children.

Whatever the situation, if parents take the initiative and open a conversation about their child's progress, it's important that you take what they say sensitively and seriously. There's a natural tendency to put people's minds at rest and to tell them there's nothing to worry about. Sometimes that is true, but when they come to you, they are clearly already worried about something, so you need to address their concerns fully, rather than brushing them off. Parents know their child very well, so listen to them carefully and take note of what they say. You don't have to commit yourself, but rather agree to look into things and get back to them when you have done so. Make a note of the conversation in your records and a note in your diary to talk to the parents again within the agreed timescale. When you have observed the child and/or discussed the matter with the class teacher, make brief notes to share with the parents. It is likely that things won't develop any further, but in this way you have laid the groundwork, just in case they do.

Involving parents formally

Formal contact can be take place during

- parents' evenings
- regular 'surgeries'
- specially arranged meetings.

Parents' evenings can present the ideal opportunity to discuss a child's progress, consider their problems and to look at targets and IEPs together. If such brief meetings (usually only 10–15 minutes) are to be effective it is important to ensure that parents have been sent any written materials (such as the IEP) beforehand. It will also help if they have been regularly kept up to date with progress and any changes in provision or personnel. This is not an occasion for surprises or revelations.

This kind of opportunity will only arise if you are not also a class teacher with your own set of parents to see when other teachers are seeing theirs. The other factor is that you may not want to have to wait for a scheduled parents' evening to review a child's progress for an IEP which finishes sooner than that. In this case, you will probably choose to fix a meeting at another time that suits you all.

You may find it is possible to set aside some time and a quiet room to hold regular 'surgeries'. These could be weekly, fortnightly, monthly or even half-termly, but the important thing is that parents of SEN children know when your surgeries are and that they are welcome either to make an appointment or just to drop in for a chat about their children.

Special meetings will need to be arranged in advance for reviews and other formal discussions. This will particularly be the case if you wish to involve outside professionals or to include a range of personnel from within the school, at a time when they are not in classrooms. Parents should always be consulted before the date and time of a formal meeting are finalised, to ensure their availability.

Handling meetings

There are several kinds of review meetings, all of which should actively involve the SEN child's parents. These include

- IEP reviews (at least termly)
- annual reviews
- transfer reviews (preparing the way for primary–secondary transfer)
- interim or emergency reviews.

Formal meetings will need appropriate preparation and organisation to make sure that they achieve optimum outcomes. Parents' participation in the education process, including meetings, must be valued and they must be supported appropriately so that, rather than feeling intimidated by the formality of such a situation, they feel empowered to contribute actively and positively to it.

Before the meeting

As soon as the meeting has been set up, parents should be sent any relevant documentation, together with some guidelines as to the purpose and format of the meeting, who will be there and how they as parents can prepare for it, for example by

- making a list of any questions they might want to ask
- writing some brief notes about anything they have noticed recently about their child's responses, attitudes or progress
- talking to their children before the meeting to gauge their views and responses to the provision that has been made for them and to ascertain any concerns they might have.

It is advisable to send a brief reminder note to parents about the date and time of the meeting a few days beforehand.

Separated parents

If parents are separated, but still share parental responsibility, make sure that they both get the same information. This can be a difficult situation and there is a risk that a degree of ill feeling may creep in if parents are not on amicable terms. It's often worth reminding them beforehand that the meeting is for the benefit of their child and it should therefore be the child's needs and well-being that are paramount. It will best help their child if they can focus their thoughts and responses on his or her needs alone, for the duration of the meeting. However, this situation will need to be approached very sensitively.

Once the meeting time and place are booked and everyone has been notified, you will find it helpful, in consultation with the class teacher, to review the child's records, any recent assessments and perhaps take a copy of one or two examples of their recent work to share with the parents at the meeting.

If anyone cannot attend the meeting, such as the educational psychologist, it will be useful to have a word with them, to see if they have any views, comments or advice to contribute to the meeting which can be reported in their absence.

If it is at all possible, the child's presence at the meeting, or for at least part of the meeting would be very beneficial. If the child will attend, parents need to know this in advance. If the child cannot or does not wish to attend, it will be helpful to ask them to make a contribution to the meeting as well. If they do not wish to make a written contribution, this could be scribed or taped instead.

At the meeting

Any official meeting will probably be a very daunting occasion for parents. It will be up to you to give the lead in setting them at ease as much as possible before the meeting itself gets under way. They will then feel more confident to take part in the meeting and it will therefore be a more productive situation.

Following these guidelines will help.

1 Welcome everyone to the meeting and thank them for coming.

2 Distribute a simple agenda.

3 Ask the parents if there are any other items they wish to add to the agenda (if they can't think of anything straight away, suggest that they can add anything they think of later in the meeting).

4 Introduce everyone who is there, or ask them to introduce themselves, together with their roles and the purpose for their participation.

5 Explain that you (or someone else) will take notes to record and clarify any discussions and decisions made, which will then be circulated to all participants afterwards.

6 Outline the purpose of the meeting and what its desired outcomes will be.

7 Begin the meeting with some positive comments about the child and their strengths (demonstrate that you know and like them – this will ease the way if you need to make any negative comments or pass on any upsetting assessment information).

8 Encourage all the professionals to speak in plain English (avoiding jargon) and to explain or illustrate their comments.

9 Invite the parents to contribute to the meeting as much as possible and to ask questions if there is anything they do not understand or agree with.

10 Listen attentively and allow brief silences to encourage parents to contribute if they wish.

11 Be open and honest, but do it sensitively when reporting on the child's progress.

12 Acknowledge the feelings and views of parents by summarising what they say at appropriate intervals, to clarify that you have understood them correctly (this will also demonstrate that you respect and value their points of view).

13 Make sure that you have copies of any reports or assessment results which you will be discussing and circulate these.

14 Put any assessment findings in context by, for example, referring to what national expectations for the child's age-group would be.

15 At the end of the meeting, summarise the main points and decisions, any action to be taken, by whom and when – repeat that this will be printed and circulated to all those present as soon as possible.

16 Thank everyone, especially the parents, for their participation.

17 Make sure that the parents leave last, so that they do not think everyone is talking about them or continuing to talk about their child after they have gone.

After the meeting

Summarise the main points of the meeting, any decisions made and any action agreed, to be circulated to all participants within a few days of the meeting. Talk to the parents as soon as possible after the meeting to check their understanding and their satisfaction with the outcomes.

Identifying needs in partnership with parents

The fact that the parents and the class teacher, probably in consultation with you as SEN coordinator, have agreed that there is a cause for concern doesn't mean that any of you have a clear idea of exactly what is wrong. You will need to provide guidance to the class teacher in the first instance as to how to support the child in the classroom and what needs to be done to ascertain what the child's difficulties may be and in what areas. Before any more accurate diagnosis can be made, it will be for you and the class teacher to develop a better understanding of the child and their general educational needs. To this end, you will need to develop a good partnership with the child's parents, who will be able to contribute valuably to this process.

You might decide to have an informal meeting with the parents. Describe briefly what you have noticed in school and why you think there may be a cause for concern. Then ask them to describe their own child, emphasising what they think are his or her strengths and weaknesses. You're looking for two things – common factors and explanations. You might find, for example, that he or she can't seem to concentrate on anything for long at school and at home is finding it difficult to cope with the changes there have recently been in family life. This process will help you to identify areas you want to follow up. Agree with the parents as to what these areas are and how you are both going to investigate them further.

After some further observations and discussions, you may then be able to select appropriate diagnostic materials or you may prefer to refer the child for professional assessment. Whatever route you follow, keep the parents informed and involved.

Handling parents' needs

Most of this chapter has been concerned with the needs of children, but the parents themselves will also have their own needs, which may require sensitive handling by you. The possibility has already been mentioned that some parents will themselves have difficulty in reading or in writing. Many parents of special needs children may well have had negative experiences themselves at school and they will bring this baggage with them into their relationships with you and the school. You will need to be aware of this and gradually allay their fears and build up their confidence to talk to you and to find ways of helping their children.

Other difficulties may also present barriers to parental participation. If a parent is blind, deaf, dumb, chronically or acutely ill or in some way disabled, this will inhibit their full participation in meetings and other in-school activities. If this is the case, it will usually be helpful to find time to make occasional home visits to keep parents informed and involved. It may even be possible to hold review meetings at their home.

It should always be remembered that parents of SEN children will inevitably find it hard at first to come to terms with their children's difficulties and need for special support. They fear what this means (perhaps that their child will be segregated from his or her peers, be labelled or bullied, or will fail at everything). They may feel guilty that their child's difficulties are in some way their fault. They will almost certainly lack confidence and will be at a loss as to how to help their child when they don't understand his or her needs, how the school's procedures work or even their own rights and responsibilities. Your support will be crucial to the parents and it will be necessary for you to explain all these things to them in plain language.

Some parents of SEN children take the opposite approach, demonstrating full confidence and detailed knowledge of their rights. Such parents may be a positive support to their children and to the school from the outset, but a few will perhaps seem or even seek to pose a threat to inexperienced or diffident class teachers and to you as SEN coordinator. A few parents may actually challenge or even confront you or other members of staff in an aggressive way.

If such a confrontation threatens or occurs, remember, first and foremost, to stay calm – this is not a personal attack on you. It will help if you can adopt the stance that it is just as well that they have chosen to vent their frustrations upon you, as you are in the best position to turn their anger round into positive participation through conciliation, understanding and support of their needs. See Chapter 8: Handling confrontation for more about how to handle this most difficult of situations

Whatever response the parents make, it will be incumbent on you to provide them with any helpful information, such as contact details for outside agencies and support groups and also the local parent partnership scheme. This scheme offers individual support and guidance through an independent parental supporter, who will work with the parents, to reassure them and guide them through the processes of assessment and target-setting.

Parents' role in statutory assessments

Schools, other agencies (such as doctors) and parents themselves are all entitled to request a statutory assessment for a child with special educational needs. If the LEA refuses to agree to the request for statutory assessment, parents have the right to appeal to the SEN and Disability Tribunal.

The statutory assessment process can be a difficult and stressful process for parents. They should be kept fully involved in the discussion leading up to the school's decision to request a statutory assessment and kept informed at every stage.

Occasionally, a school may suggest that the parents themselves request a statutory assessment to take place. This will probably be because it may be more likely to take place if the parents make such a request – the LEA must comply with the parents' request 'unless they conclude, upon examining all the evidence provided to them, that a statutory assessment is not necessary.' (DfES, 2001 – 7:21).

It will obviously be in everyone's interest, whoever makes the actual request or referral, to put together a comprehensive and fully documented case. At the school, this will be your responsibility. However, the parents will also be invited to submit a report. They may find this a daunting, difficult and even a painful proposition. Often, parents will find it hard to achieve an appropriate balance. Writing too positively will weaken their child's case but being brutally honest and detailed in writing about their child's difficulties is very hard for parents.

With your guidance and practical help they will realise that it is in their child's best interests to provide honest, clear and relevant information (even if it does seem very negative) and they will be able to feel more confident in making a strong case. Parents may also need to make some other preparation, such as investigating local secondary or special school provision. They will be glad of your support in helping them to make informed choices.

When it comes to the report you make on the child's needs, as part of the statutory assessment process, it's a good idea to share this with their parents. They will see it later anyway, so it's best that they have time to discuss it with you and that they don't have to deal with any shocks or surprises in an official document.

If the LEA does go ahead with the statutory assessment, the parents will receive a draft statement of special educational need. They might well want to discuss this document with you and it will probably be helpful if you can take them through it, explaining any jargon and specific recommendations.

Finally

While nearly all schools value the partnerships they develop with their pupils' parents, when children are identified as having special educational needs, such close cooperation is even more crucial in achieving the best provision possible for their children. As SEN coordinator, you will lead this closer partnership and from it will be better able to ensure that IEPs are well targeted and provision is the best it can be.

Passing on your skills and expertise is also an important factor. Make sure that your staff feel well supported and that you are able to pass on to them the kinds of communication skills which will help them handle the parent partnership on a daily basis.

Reference

DfES (2001) *Special Educational Needs Code of Practice.* Ref: 581/2001. London: DfES.

Thanks to Robin Bartlett, Sue Byron and Eithne Leming for their contributions to this chapter.

CHAPTER 8
Handling confrontation

SEN provision is mainly concerned with people's needs, wishes and emotions. These are all sensitive areas and anyone who works with children who have special educational needs knows that there is always the possibility of a mild disagreement turning into a major dispute. Confrontation can be very damaging for the well-being of any child in the long term.

As SEN coordinator you need to know how to deal with confrontational situations such as

- parents who are unhappy with provision, progress, etc.

- colleagues who don't want to work in the way you suggest

- support or other groups who sometimes encourage parents to expect more than you are able to provide.

The two important skills that will help you with these potentially awkward situations are assertiveness and negotiation. We'll take a closer look at these skills later in this chapter.

How to deal with confrontational situations

It is easy to imagine that all confrontation is harmful and should be avoided at all costs. This is not the case. Confrontation can have a beneficial and positive effect by

- getting things out in the open and clearing the air

- breaking a deadlock

- challenging the *status quo*

- proving that you mean business.

For many people though, confrontation can be difficult, painful and unproductive. It often ends in a lose/lose scenario. There are some very good reasons to learn how to avoid too much confrontation.

Negative results of conflict include

- a polarisation of views which leads to entrenchment

- victimisation

- isolation

- resentment that can permanently damage personal and professional relationships.

The best way to deal with a confrontational situation is to spot it coming. Understanding and accounting for the behaviour of others is one of the most effective methods of defusing confrontation. It's necessary to step outside your own feelings for a moment and try to empathise with the other person. Empathy is a difficult concept, especially when you don't know the other person well. It's important to think about the other person's situation and feelings before committing yourself to certain actions. Once you have embraced the idea of empathetic listening, you will feel more able to deal with potential confrontation.

Our tendency to react emotionally to another person's statement by forming an evaluation of it from our own point of view was once described by Carl Rogers as 'The major barrier to interpersonal communication'. (Rogers, 1967 – p331)

Another good idea is to try to resolve a conflict by using a recognised dispute resolution process. There are a number of these that are often very similar to systematic problem solving techniques. An example is given in the box opposite.

Confrontation with dissatisfied parents

For the vast majority of parents, their child is the most precious and protected thing imaginable. Parents of children with special educational needs often see their own child's problems in a way that, for an outsider, appears to be out of all reasonable proportion. Failure to understand their point of view can anger parents.

Angry parents can be intimidating and so the first piece of advice is to stay calm whenever you can. Also remember to seek the help of your colleagues if things do appear to be getting out of hand.

If you are caught up in an ongoing confrontation with a parent, try the systematic conflict analysis the

Conflict analysis

Photocopy the blank form on page 106 and fill it in as honestly as you can, from your own point of view.

- **Box 1** – (make sure you have the correctly numbered box – the second one down on the left) write a sentence that describes your perception of the conflict.

- **Box 2** – write a list of all the things (including people) that are contributing to the problem.

- **Box 3** – describe what you think things would be like if you took no direct action to resolve the conflict. What would the consequences be if you went off on long-term sick leave for example?

- **Box 4** – try to think of a possible solution, the 'if only' dream that would resolve the conflict. Write it as a short sentence.

- **Box 5** – this is similar to box 2. Write a bullet point list of the contributors (people and things) that would, in your view, contribute to the possible solution.

- **Box 6** – fill in a description of what life would be like for you, the parent and the child if the solution in box 5 actually worked. What would the consequences be in say six months or a year?

Now (and this is the really useful part of the exercise) test your skill at empathising, by doing the whole exercise again, only this time describing someone else's perception of the problem in box 1. It won't be the same as yours. As you complete the other boxes, try to imagine the other person's feelings about the conflict. If it is a parent, feelings of protection for their child will be very high.

Compare your own analysis and proposed solutions for the confrontation with the one you have completed for the other person.

- Where are the important differences?

- What can be done to bring all sides closer together?

Now look again at your own completed boxes and ask yourself some other questions.

- Have you included yourself as a contributor in box 2?

- Are the contributors in box 2 the same as in box 5? If not, with whom do you need to work in order to achieve a resolution?

- How do the consequences in box 3 compare with box 6? If they are not too different, then ask yourself if it is really worth trying to achieve a solution. It might be better to learn to live with the situation.

box above to help you think clearly about the causes and solutions.

Finally, when trying to resolve or prevent confrontation with parents, don't forget to use the most effective method of all – listening. Sometimes, parents just need someone who will really listen to their views. Show you are paying attention by using good eye contact, appropriate facial expressions, gestures such as nods, repeating phrases or paraphrasing and open questions. The best listeners to complainants manage to give the impression that the other party is absolutely right to come and inform the listener and agrees that it is necessary to address the complaint in some way. Always try to close a discussion by summarising the key points you have heard in a sincere and optimistic manner. Then agree on a specific target, such as meeting again to review the situation together in a month's time.

Confrontation with colleagues

The headteacher and governors have a proper expectation that you will carry out certain duties as SEN coordinator – some of them are statutory requirements. These are not always fully appreciated by other members of staff who have their own

responsibilities to worry about. Trying to convince staff about the necessity of certain SEN requirements can create tension and confrontation.

Much of what applies to the resolution of conflicts with parents can also be applied to confrontation with colleagues. The conflict resolution prompt, for example, is useful in any confrontational situation. You could go a step further by introducing this approach to your colleagues and working through it jointly.

When dealing with difficult colleagues, try to remember that there is a need here to differentiate between manipulation, motivation and persuasion.

- You are manipulating someone if your own motives are flawed or deceitful.

- You are motivating colleagues, often through persuasion, if your motives are honest and in the best interests of the children.

Confrontation with support groups and other agencies

Sometimes you will find that parents have had dealings with support groups who, with all the best intentions, have led them to expect more than you

Conflict resolution prompt

2 Factors contributing to the problem	5 Factors which could contribute to the solution
1 My perception of the conflict	4 The ideal solution
3 Consequences (without resolution)	6 The short/long-term consequences if the ideal solution worked

are able to provide. Occasionally this can lead to confrontation with the support group itself.

When dealing with groups rather than individuals, you need to think about the group dynamics. Every group has its own chemistry, which is a direct result of the individual personalities and characteristics that comprise the group.

Dealing with confrontational groups requires some of the skills of a public relations officer.

- Find out who the influential members of the group are (not always the chair or leader).

- Meet personally with the influencers as soon as you can.

- Listen very carefully to their views and show your understanding.

- Use every opportunity possible to show that you share their aims and want to move forward.

- Don't forget to spread the good news by celebrating children's achievements.

- If you have to give some difficult messages, emphasise any positive aspects.

- If you have made a genuine mistake, offer a sincere apology to the group.

The last point is especially important. An apology can be a very powerful method of defusing confrontation with a group if delivered in the right way at the right time.

Assertiveness

Assertiveness is behaviour designed to obtain your reasonable rights with dignity while respecting the dignity and rights of others. When you are being assertive, you should feel relaxed and confident. Your eye contact is strong and you display positive body language. You should be accepting of other people's emotions but very aware of your own feelings. Assertiveness means being well-informed but not bossy. Assertive behaviour is very important if you want to make an impact and establish your credibility.

Some people think they are being assertive when they are actually being aggressive. Aggression is the most infectious of behaviours. Aggression can be very subtle and almost imperceptible but once detected does nothing to reduce the anxiety levels in a confrontation. Find out all you can about assertive behaviour and practise using it in a safe environment such as a staff meeting, for example, where a trusted colleague observes your level of assertive behaviour

and gives you feedback using the definition given above. They can also make a judgement about whether you have strayed over the line into aggressiveness. You don't have to go on courses to develop your personal assertiveness skills but it might help if you do have difficulty in this important area.

Are you an effective negotiator?

Experienced SEN coordinators will know how important negotiation skills are in the normal course of their job. Use the following checklist to assess your own skills in this area and seek further professional development opportunities if you feel you need them.

- Do you understand what is meant by a win/win outcome?   Yes/No

- Are you normally willing to compromise in order to solve problems?   Yes/No

- Are you able to think creatively and flexibly to generate solutions?   Yes/No

- Can you name the benefits of at least six different types of questioning?   Yes/No

- Do you have both stamina and patience in stressful situations?   Yes/No

- Are you able to empathise with others' points of view?   Yes/No

- Do others regard you as a good listener?   Yes/No

If you registered five or more 'Yes' answers to the questions above, you are a natural negotiator. Less than five may mean that you have more to learn about effective negotiating.

Finally

Preventing confrontations and resolving conflicts are very important facets of your role. It is an area that requires much common sense and some specific skills. These skills are not difficult to learn but they do require commitment and practice. Once acquired, substantial benefits accrue to staff, parents and, most important of all, the children.

Reference

Rogers, C (1967) *On Becoming a Person*. London: Constable.

Thanks to Jim Laing for his major contribution to this chapter.

CHAPTER 9
Working with governors

School governing bodies have various responsibilities relating to children with special educational needs and the provision the school makes for them. For most of these responsibilities, governors rely on both you, as SEN coordinator, and the headteacher, either to act on their behalf or to provide them with information and advice as appropriate. It is in everybody's interests that you all understand each other's roles and responsibilities and that you develop ways of working well together.

The 2001 SEN Code of Practice states that

> 'Governing bodies should, with the head teacher, decide the school's general policy and approach to meeting pupils' special educational needs for those with and without statements. They must set up appropriate staffing and funding arrangements and oversee the school's work.' (DfES, 2001 – 1:16)

Clearly governors shouldn't – and can't – do this in isolation. They need you to provide information and guidance. The governing body carries the final responsibility, but governors employ you to help them meet that responsibility.

Governors' role and responsibilities

Governors have a strategic role and a monitoring role. They are responsible for ensuring that appropriate policies and procedures are in place and that they are being used to fulfil the school's overall aim of providing high standards of education for all of its children. The Code of Practice reiterates the main aspects of the role, which are familiar to all experienced governors.

1 With the headteacher and the SEN coordinator, decide on the school's policy and approach to children with special educational needs. This should cover children with or without statements.

2 Report to the parents, annually, on the nature and effect of the school's policy for SEN.

3 Work within the legal requirements of the Education Act 1996: section 317, which states that governors must ensure that the necessary provision is in place for children with special educational needs.

4 Ensure that the school is managed in such a way that high standards for all of its children, including those with SEN, can be promoted. (The School Standards and Framework Act 1998)

5 When setting targets for the headteacher, as part of the performance management framework for the school, make sure that objectives include children with SEN.

6 Ensure that the school has a 'responsible person' to see that the children with SEN receive their full entitlement and that all staff are aware of these needs. This role may be delegated to the head, or possibly to the SEN governor.

7 During the process of school self-review, ensure that systems are in place to keep governors informed about the impact of the policy for SEN in the school, the use of delegated funding and the quality of provision.

In practice, many of these duties will be delegated to the SEN governor.

In 2002 the Disability Code of Practice made explicit two further duties for which the governors will be responsible. These are

1 the duty not to treat children less favourably

2 the duty to make reasonable adjustments for disabled children.

Governors won't normally be directly involved in the day-to-day activities of and support for children with special educational needs. Their role is to have an overview of what happens so that they can be confident that SEN children are fully included and are being given the attention they need.

To fulfil its own role the governing body needs to be

• aware of what goes on in the school

• aware of current requirements

• sure that appropriate resources are available

• sure that its policies are being implemented.

Confidentiality

As SEN coordinator, you have access to a great deal of information about individual children. This information – including statements of special educational need – is confidential and can only be made available to parents and those professionals who need to see it.

Governors shouldn't normally be involved in the details of the special educational needs of individual children. They don't have access to the confidential records.

The exceptions to this are when parents ask the governing body to intervene in some way – such as to deal with a complaint. On these occasions it is the governing body – or sometimes a committee of that body or the SEN governor – that has access to the information, rather than individual governors.

The SEN governor (or committee)

The governing body has an umbrella role concerning special educational needs provision in the school. To carry out this role efficiently it can delegate elements of its responsibilities to an SEN governor, or to an SEN committee. Some governing bodies have an SEN committee and then appoint one of its members as SEN governor.

If it is decided to have an SEN committee, it has to be set up formally and be given clear terms of reference. In some schools special educational needs is part of the responsibility of the governing body's curriculum committee.

Responsibilities

The SEN governor or committee might be responsible for

- drafting and reviewing the school's SEN policy
- gathering information about the way the policy is put into action and its success in terms of its effect on the education of the children
- monitoring the practical implications of the policy – considering such things as the accessibility of the buildings and resources so that all children can take a full part in the life of the school
- participating in the budgeting process to ensure sufficient funding for SEN provision in the school
- ensuring that the admissions policy is implemented fairly with regard to any prospective SEN or disabled children

- reporting to the full governing body on a regular basis
- drafting the section on special educational needs to be included in the governing body's annual report to parents.

Complaints

The responsibility for dealing with any issues raised through the complaints procedure about the workings of the policy cannot be handled by the SEN governor alone. Complaints made to governors must always be handled by an appropriate committee. It will be up to the governors of a particular school to decide how this is to be managed.

A designated SEN governor

Most schools delegate ongoing responsibilities to a designated SEN governor, rather than a committee. The advantage of appointing an individual SEN governor is that there is one point of contact.

Many schools find that the SEN governor takes a real and constructive interest in what happens in the school. They can act as a sounding board and can be particularly informed and supportive when SEN issues are discussed in meetings of the full governing body.

A well-informed SEN governor can be a powerful advocate for special educational needs. They can make sure that the governing body is kept up to date and is aware of the issues facing the school.

Fulfilling the role

The role of the SEN governor is chiefly one of liaison. They gather information from the school, pass information to the school and report to the SEN committee and/or the governing body. To fulfil the role, the SEN governor needs to

- visit the school, particularly to see children at work in class and in any support groups
- talk with you as SEN coordinator, and to other staff including class teachers, the headteacher and any specialist staff
- gather information about the number of children on School Action or School Action Plus, the range of needs and specialist provision
- know about the resources and facilities available for children with special educational needs
- attend training courses and other meetings for SEN governors

- keep up-to-date about any new regulations or proposals
- produce reports for the full governing body.

This role is one which needs to be filled by someone who not only has an understanding of children's needs but who can also be diplomatic and professional and who will respect the sensitive nature of what they see and hear.

The responsible person

Each school is meant to have a 'responsible person' whose role is to liaise between the school and the LEA. In particular, the responsible person

- receives information from the LEA when a child has been given a statement of special educational need or when a child with a statement moves from another school
- makes sure that the child's teachers know about his or her special educational needs
- endorses any request the school makes for a child to be given a statutory assessment.

The responsible person has to be either the chair of the governing body, another governor or the headteacher. In most schools it makes sense for the headteacher to take the role, but the decision should be formally made and minuted by the full governing body. Whoever is made responsible person it is very likely that you, as SEN coordinator will actually be involved in all the communications.

The communication chain

The various people involved in monitoring provision and delivering the education for those children with special educational needs have a duty to report back to the full governing body. How they do this will depend upon the size of the school, the numbers of staff involved and the level of provision they need to make. Another factor relates to the way in which the governors' responsibilities have been shared out.

In general, the chain of communication – modified to suit the actual organisation of the particular school – is likely to look like the diagram below.

Alongside this chain are outside professionals and agencies and the local education authority. Liaison with these bodies will usually be directly through you, as SEN coordinator, and occasionally with the headteacher, class teachers or teaching assistants.

A programme of communication

When the above process is carried out systematically each term, the governing body fulfils its statutory responsibilities in an efficient and effective way. Governors are always informed and fully aware of the current situation so that they can make any necessary decisions for change.

In a well-run system, small adaptations are easily managed and there will rarely be a need for major changes.

- The child, their parents or carers, teaching assistants and the class teacher inform the SEN coordinator about progress when they review the IEP and contribute to the target-setting process.
- The SEN coordinator collates information for the child's records and for internal auditing purposes. This information, or a summary of it, may also be passed to the headteacher. Copies of new IEPs will need to be passed to the class teacher, support teacher and teaching assistants.
- The SEN coordinator, together with teaching assistants and possibly the headteacher, evaluate this information and draw from it any conclusions about changes in provision that need to be made, either for individual children or for the school as a whole.
- The SEN coordinator reports this information in outline form (not generally naming individuals) to the SEN governor. Together they identify areas of success and how they were achieved and consider whether there needs to be any strategic plan for change.
- The SEN governor reports back to the SEN committee. Together they discuss any proposed changes, and agree on further action.

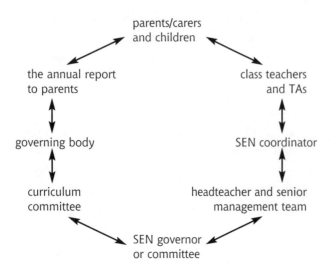

Ten key ways of working with governors

1   Arrange to meet the SEN governor (or committee) at least once a term.

2   Provide the SEN governor with jargon-free reading matter about developments in special educational needs and with details of any relevant training courses.

3   Provide regular written reports on your own activities and those of any other SEN staff to the SEN governor or committee.

4   Provide information on the number of children on School Action or School Action Plus, (including early years if appropriate) to the SEN governor and, through them, to the full governing body each term.

    Also provide updates regarding the overall attainment and progress of SEN children whenever such data becomes available.

5   Whenever governors visit classes, make sure they are aware of children with special educational needs and how their needs are being met.

6   Invite governors to see any withdrawal or special groups in operation.

7   If you are not a governor, ask to be invited to meetings of the SEN or curriculum committee and to those parts of full governing body meetings where SEN provision is being evaluated and discussed.

    You may be asked to make a presentation to the governing body. If so, be well prepared – ready to answer questions and justify any statements you make. Have information available (perhaps handouts or OHTs).

8   Make sure that governors are aware of the resources you have for special educational needs and how they are used.

9   Make sure governors know how you make use of any learning support teachers and the school's teaching assistants.

10 Inform the governors' budget allocation process. If you need extra funding at any time, explain carefully what resources you need, why you need them and how they will be used.

- The SEN governor or committee reports to the full governing body of the school about what has been done and on any proposals they have drawn up. They recommend that the full governing body ratify any proposed changes to the policy or the provision for special educational needs.

The SEN budget

One of the governors' responsibilities is to provide an appropriate budget allocation for SEN provision and an accompanying duty is to ensure that the school provides value for money in all its expenditure. Having made a budget allocation for SEN, they will need to monitor both the expenditure and its effect.

To help governors to come to funding decisions, in which they have to balance the needs and requests of all departments of the school, it will be helpful if you can meet with the headteacher to put together a costed bid for funding. This will need to take account of expected needs during the coming year (including staffing and other professional advice) and additional resourcing requests, preferably in prioritised order.

In order to help them monitor value for money, you will need to tell governors about

- how much money has been spent

- what it has been spent on

- how expenditure so far compares with expectations in the budget profile

- any information related to success criteria, if these have been set

- any changes in circumstances which are likely to affect funding needs.

SEN in the governors' annual report

Each year the governing body should use its report to parents to provide information on SEN, including

- the success of the school's SEN policy
- any significant changes to the policy
- any consultations with the LEA or other schools
- any local or national SEN initiatives or legislation and how it has affected the school's provision
- numbers of children on School Action and School Action Plus (including early years if appropriate)
- summary information about staffing levels and roles
- special SEN training undertaken by the SEN coordinator, class teachers or teaching assistants
- the allocation of funding and resources.

In producing their report, governors will look to you for information and guidance. You will already have given them, mainly through the SEN governor, much of the information they need during the course of the year, but it is likely that they will want you to summarise that information and to provide additional detail. This is a good opportunity for you to produce your own annual report for governors, even though not everything will make its way into their final report to parents.

Finally

Governors have statutory duties relating to special educational needs. However seriously they take these duties, they can only accomplish many of them through the activities of other people. You have a key role, not only in the day-to-day implementation of the governing body's SEN policy, but also in reporting to governors on that implementation. They need the information that you are able to provide, so it's up to you to work with them to provide it in the most effective, accurate and accessible way possible. In this way, working with governors can become a rewarding exercise, which encourages and enables their active support for the future well-being of SEN provision in your school.

Reference

DfES (2001) *Special Educational Needs Code of Practice.* Ref. 581/2001. London: DfES.

Thanks to Lynn Cousins and Graham Reeves for their contributions to this chapter.

CHAPTER 10

The early years

Since the National Childcare Strategy was launched in 1998 to expand childcare services, there have been a number of moves to make sure that all types of pre-school and Foundation Stage provision offer good-quality care and education in the early years for all children, including those with special needs.

This chapter considers the impact of all these new requirements and developments on the role of the SEN coordinator. Pre-school and Foundation Stage provision is examined, together with the main strands of diversity in this area, followed by the 'graduated approach' to SEN identification and intervention and related aspects of assessment, transition, liaison and multi-agency working.

The Foundation Stage

The Foundation Stage includes all children from ages three to five. For many children of this age, the early education setting will provide their first experience of learning with a peer group. The government's Early Learning Goals set out what is expected of children at the Foundation Stage in six areas of learning, which are

- personal, social and emotional
- communication, language and literacy
- mathematical development
- knowledge and understanding of the world
- physical development
- creative development.

By the age of five, most children will have achieved these early milestones, but some will still be working towards them. While this could be an indication that a child has special educational needs, there may be factors which have delayed or hampered their readiness for learning at this stage, so it should not be assumed that this is an SEN child. However such children, whether or not they are designated as having special educational needs, will need carefully differentiated learning opportunities to help them progress, together with regular and frequent monitoring of their progress. Indeed, this approach

may well have the effect of pre-empting any need for more prolonged intervention and support at a later stage.

National Standards

In 1999 the government decided that day care providers for children under the age of eight would be regulated by the Early Years Directorate, which is part the Office for Standards in Education (Ofsted). The new *National Standards for Under Eights Day Care and Childminding* were written to give guidance to all providers of day care and represent the criteria by which they will be inspected and regulated. The National Standards came into effect in September 2001.

The 2001 SEN Code of Practice emphasises the importance of Early Years Development and Childcare Partnerships (EYDCPs) in bringing together private, voluntary and independent providers with LEAs, Social Services departments, health services and parent representatives to plan services in the early education sector.

Early education providers include mainstream primary, nursery and special schools, as well as day nurseries, family centres, portage schemes, independent schools and nurseries, playgroups and other pre-schools. Childminders are also now a recognised part of this group. All of these providers of early education must now have a written SEN policy and follow the National Standards.

What are the National Standards?

The National Standards

'...represent a baseline of quality below which no provider may fall. However, they are also intended to underpin a continuous improvement in quality in all settings.' (DfEE, 2001)

The five modules presented in the Standards are

1 childminding
2 crèches
3 full day care
4 out-of-school care
5 sessional care.

Each module reflects a different type of childcare provision and contains the same uniform headings. There are 14 such headings with each Standard, describing particular outcomes relating to the specific module and the criteria by which these outcomes can be achieved.

Standard 10 – special needs

All early years providers must have a registered person who

> '...is aware that some children may have special needs and is proactive in ensuring that appropriate action can be taken when such a child is identified or admitted to the provision.' (DfEE, 2001)

Standard 10 states that the registered person who offers pre-school provision must be aware of the criteria for the identification and assessment of children with special needs as set out in the Code of Practice and

- produce a written statement for parents detailing the provision they make for children with special educational needs and disabilities
- ensure that staffing arrangements and the physical environment meet the needs of individuals and groups of children with specific learning difficulties
- ensure the principle of inclusion is maintained with facilities, activities and play opportunities being provided for all children where reasonably possible
- ensure privacy for children who may need more intimate care.
- Liaison with parents is an important part of this Standard. The registered person is expected to consult with parents about the need for special services and equipment for their children.

Pre-school provision

As SEN coordinator you will need to be aware of the full range and different types of early years provision available in your region in order to develop effective communication and transition systems. The opportunities for pre-school provision available in most LEAs are

- playgroups
- nursery schools
- pre-schools
- childminders
- opportunity groups
- portage.

In some priority areas there are also such initiatives as Early Excellence Centres, Sure Start schemes and other EYDCPs.

Early Excellence Centres

The diversity of pre-school provision can make liaison between services difficult. In some areas centres have been designated and funded by the government to provide integrated childcare, health, social services and education for children under five, including those with special needs. These centres also run education and training programmes to develop parenting, employment and other skills. The aim of these centres is to provide models of good practice in integrated early years provision and to improve cooperation between parents or carers and teachers and other professionals. Liaison between Early Excellence Centres and the schools they feed is a great improvement on former arrangements.

Early Years Development and Childcare Partnerships

As explained above, EYDCPs bring together the whole range of providers of early years education and care. These partnerships are expected to draw on exemplars from Early Excellence Centres when developing integrated education and childcare provision.

Playgroups

These groups usually offer pre-school sessions of 2–3 hours (either mornings or afternoons) during term time. Each group has a registered leader who is responsible for making provision for children with learning difficulties. Many children with special needs attend their local playgroup. These groups offer a wide range of play activities and most of the activities can be enjoyed by all children regardless of their ability. You will need to work together with your early years coordinator to develop close links with local playgroups. Wherever possible, it is useful for you, as SEN coordinator, to make visits to your local playgroups in order to observe any children who may have been identified as having special educational needs and who are due to attend your school. You will also find it helpful to talk to the playgroup leaders and any other relevant professionals.

Nursery schools

Nursery schools provide care for children from a very young age. Many are run privately and are quite expensive. Some are subsidised by companies for their employees. Others are attached to or based in local mainstream schools. They usually provide half or full day care and education for children under five. You will need to make contact with the registered person at any feeder nursery school during the summer term if you know that a child with special needs is due to transfer to the Reception class of your school.

Pre-schools

If your school offers pre-school places to local children you may have some children with learning difficulties already in your care. As SEN coordinator, you will be expected to

- collect, record and update relevant information about each child's needs
- liaise with parents and relevant professionals
- advise and support the early years coordinator/ pre-school leader/Reception teacher
- help write practical and effective IEPs.

Childminders

Childminders are self-employed and look after children in their own home. They have to be approved and registered by social services. Some have a specific interest in children with disabilities and can provide a flexible and personal service. External support services may contact you prior to a child starting school if they are receiving support through Early Years Action Plus.

Specialist SEN early years providers

In addition to the mainstream early years providers, there are a number oriented specifically towards children with special needs.

Opportunity groups

Opportunity groups for pre-school children with special educational needs developed in the late 1970s. They are often based within or attached to a child development centre, family centre, voluntary organisation or some other existing provision. Many opportunity groups are run by the Pre-School Learning Alliance.

Opportunity groups make special provision for a significant proportion of children with disabilities or special educational needs, but they sometimes include other children with no special educational needs. The emphasis is on inclusion, with additional support if necessary. All opportunity and special

interest groups work closely with parents and have strong links with community and support services (especially the LEA, health and social services).

Each group has a qualified teacher, plus play leaders and a management committee. Opportunity groups provide play activities and therapy for children with special needs and can take children from an early age. Some opportunity groups, particularly if they are attached to health settings, may be used as observation and assessment centres, as well as for developmental play activities. Parents can ask for help and advice from a wide range of professionals as well as meeting other parents in similar situations.

The children who attend opportunity groups have their progress monitored through Early Years Action Plus. This means that there has been involvement by external support services, who will have helped with advice on IEPs, provided specialist assessments or loaned specific equipment.

As SEN coordinator of the child's receiving school, you will need to maintain close links with the opportunity group leader in order to ensure continuity of SEN provision.

Portage

If a child's special needs are identified at an early age, their parents may receive help from the Portage scheme. Portage is an educational home-visiting service for pre-school children whose development is significantly delayed.

Portage has, for many years, been the most widely used form of assessment and support for pre-school children with special needs. It was developed in the town of Portage in the US in the early 1970s.

In the Portage programme, the needs of a pre-school child are assessed. Then a team works with the parents to build on the abilities the child already has, as well as teaching them new skills. The system is designed to be both carefully structured and flexible in order to help parents become effective teachers of their own children. It is based on four main activities.

1 Weekly home visits (by a trained home visitor).
2 Weekly written teaching activities (designed for each individual child).
3 Teaching and recording (carried out by the child's parent/s).
4 Weekly supervision of the home visitor.

Multidisciplinary Portage teams are made up of home-visitors who are trained in Portage methods and have extensive experience in working with special needs children and their families. They may be teachers, speech or occupational therapists, nursery nurses, social workers or other volunteers with relevant experience.

When parents enrol with a Portage scheme through their LEA, their child's current development is observed and assessed, using a checklist of 624 behaviours, which are divided into six areas of development.

- Infant stimulation.
- Socialisation.
- Self-help.
- Cognitive development.
- Motor development.
- Language.

The focus of Portage is always on the positive – discovering what a child can do and then building on those skills through specially designed activities.

As SEN coordinator of the child's receiving school, you should be contacted by the educational psychologist if a child is on the Portage programme, well ahead of their transfer to your school.

The value of early intervention

Extensive research has been undertaken in the US in recent years into the effects of early intervention for children with special needs and difficult backgrounds. The findings of this research have shown that

'...early childhood interventions can yield substantial advantages to recipients in terms of emotional and cognitive development, education, economic well-being and health.' (Karoly et al., 1998)

The Code of Practice states that

'The importance of early identification, assessment and provision for any child who may have special educational needs cannot be over emphasised. The earlier action is taken, the more responsive the child is likely to be, and the more readily can intervention be made without undue disruption to the organisation of the school.' (DfES, 2001)

Graduated approach to identification and intervention

The Code of Practice advises a graduated response to young children's needs in both the pre-school and early school environment. It's important that all

children's progress is monitored through continuous assessment at the Foundation Stage. The government's early learning goals represent what most children will achieve by the time they reach Year 1 of primary education and should form the basis for assessment. If a child is not making progress or has a specific difficulty then the pre-school provider needs to begin intervention through Early Years Action.

The DfES, in partnership with the Coram Family Foundation, published a very useful document entitled *Intervening Early* in 2002. This document provides a framework for early intervention, at any stage from age 2 to the end of the primary years. It provides excellent checklists for use by an SEN coordinator in identifying and addressing a child's special needs. It also includes some particularly useful checklists of risk factors and symptoms of distress for use to assess children of all ages.

Early Years Action

Many young children with difficulties respond well to a range of pre-school activities and differentiated approaches to learning. However, some children may need intervention through Early Years Action. At this stage pre-school providers are expected to monitor a child's progress through an IEP. In consultation with their parents or carers, the child's difficulties should be discussed and a few short-term targets set. At least one of these targets could become the responsibility of the parents or carers.

As SEN coordinator at the receiving primary school, if a child already has an IEP on arrival in the Reception class, you must ensure that the targets are reviewed and new targets set during the first term of the child's entry to the school.

Early Years Action Plus

Some children may need more specific help and the advice of external support services may be needed. These children may

- speak English as an additional language
- have specific communication difficulties
- have sensory or physical difficulties
- have emotional or behavioural difficulties
- have made little or no progress in particular areas of development
- have general learning difficulties.

At this stage, pre-school providers are expected to monitor a child's progress through a more detailed

IEP. In consultation with parents and carers and professionals from the relevant support services, specific targets should be set and reviewed regularly. You will need to ensure that the targets are reviewed and new targets set within the first term of the child's entry to primary school.

Assessment

If a pre-school, nursery or Reception child is identified as having special educational needs, it is the result of a team approach, following a number of professionals and the child's parents sharing their findings and progress reports over a period of time and reaching a consensus of opinion and recommendations about the child's needs.

Identifying the special needs of children in the early years is often a complex process and requires a range of different approaches from those conventionally used in schools. The assessment tools and procedures used with school-aged children are usually not appropriate for use with younger ones. Most of any assessment and identification carried out will be through observing early years children at play.

Play is, of course, vitally important to all children's learning. Purposeful play that reflects or slightly stretches the current abilities of the child is best, using interesting and appropriate materials in a supportive environment where children can develop at their own pace. You may find it helpful to recommend particular types of play situations and materials for the teacher or parents to use with children who appear to be having difficulties.

Children need to

- manipulate objects
- look for challenges in using materials
- interact with others.

Most children with special educational needs have trouble with one or more of these areas. Observing children and recording their performance over time will provide a useful basis to help you identify their difficulties and their needs and to plan for their progress, in small steps.

The early years observation summary on page 118 provides a possible format for recording observations and initial assessments, based on the six areas of the Early Learning Goals. The aim is to gather information about the child to inform future planning and prioritise areas for targets on an IEP. It can also be used to identify areas for further and more detailed

observation or assessment and as the basis for discussions with parents or carers and other professionals.

Once a child is in the Reception class at school, baseline assessment outcomes can be very useful towards the assessment and identification of a child's special educational needs.

It is crucial that parents or carers are involved at every stage of the process, from the assessment and identification of a child's needs, to the targets set and the level and nature of the support provided.

Lines of communication

As SEN coordinator, you will need to make sure that effective liaison prior to a child starting primary school is available to parents, carers, children, pre-school leaders and relevant professionals. It's important that lines of communication are clear and give opportunities for the exchange of useful and essential information. You may have developed effective communication systems in partnership with your early years coordinator. These could include

- assessment liaison meetings
- federation, pyramid or cluster group meetings
- multi-professional consultation meetings
- visits to pre-school settings
- planned familiarisation visits to school
- home visits
- visits from support service professionals

Assessment liaison meetings

Records of continuous assessment should be shared between pre-school providers and early years coordinators in primary schools. One of the most effective ways of sharing can be through an assessment liaison meeting. This meeting can be held early in the summer term, specifically for the sharing of continuous assessment records including IEPs. As SEN coordinator you should take part in these meetings alongside your early years coordinator so that you can talk about those children who have been monitored through Early Years Action or Action Plus.

Federation, pyramid or cluster group meetings

All providers of government-funded early years education are expected to have a written SEN policy and to make graduated responses to the needs of children with learning difficulties, in accordance with

Early years observation summary

Child's name .... **D.o.b.** ....

Admission date .... **Home language** ....

Areas where observations show help is needed	What actions and outcomes so far?
Personal, social and emotional	
Communication, language and literacy	
Mathematical development	
Knowledge and understanding of the world	
Physical development	
Creative development	
What are the child's interests and strengths?	
What are the parents' or carers' views?	
What outside agencies are involved (if any)? (Attach reports if appropriate.)	

Signature (SEN coordinator) .... **Date** ....

Signatures (parents/carers) ....

.... **Date** ....

the Code of Practice. Partnerships between primary schools and early years providers can be particularly supportive when developing SEN policies and practices.

In some LEAs, groups of schools and pre-school providers arrange regular meetings to share best practice and discuss early years and special needs issues. Support services are often invited to give advice on particular concerns. These meetings give opportunities for regular liaison between pre-school providers and primary schools and ensure continuity of provision.

Multi-professional consultation meetings

Some LEAs organise pre-school multi-professional consultation meetings prior to a child moving to primary school. As SEN coordinator, you would be invited to these meetings. Children who have attended opportunity groups, have received help through Portage or have had their progress monitored through Early Years Action Plus are usually the subject of such meetings. Parents are invited to contribute alongside those adults and other professionals who have been involved with their child. These transfer meetings are arranged specifically to discuss individual children's needs and to ensure continuity of special needs provision.

Visits to pre-school settings

Early years coordinators usually make visits to local pre-school settings to observe children. It will be useful for you, as SEN coordinator, to arrange to accompany your early years coordinator on at least one such visit, or to arrange a visit of your own, especially to observe children who have already been identified as having special needs and who are due to transfer to your school.

Planned familiarisation visits to school

Most primary schools organise a programme of planned visits for pre-school children and parents in the term prior to starting school, or sometimes over a longer period of time, especially if the pre-school provision is on-site. Early years teachers and the SEN coordinator from the primary school often make an initial visit to each pre-school so that the children can meet them in a familiar setting. When the children and parents visit the primary school, the parents meet together while the children take part in a range of activities with their new teachers. It's a good idea to ask the registered person from each pre-school group to attend on one of the days. Informal discussion with children, parents and staff can take place on these visits and help towards smooth transition from one phase to the next.

Home visits

Some parents or childminders may be unable to attend meetings or make school visits. If a child is receiving support through Early Years Action Plus, it's important that you work together with your early years coordinator to ensure that liaison time is made available. You may need to offer home visits at a time convenient to both parents and childminders. It may also be beneficial to invite the local parent partnership representative, SEN case worker or social worker to come along, or if necessary an interpreter. Although home visits are time consuming, they do give you the opportunity to observe the child in their most familiar environment and to talk about their needs in more detail.

Visits from support service professionals

Liaison with the support services is essential if a child has been monitored through Early Years Action Plus or has a statement of special educational need. The professionals who have been working with the child will have contributed to his or her IEP and will want to work towards a smooth transition to school. It's a good idea to arrange visits when all those school staff who will be working with the child are present. The support services will give advice on how to use equipment and suggest teaching strategies and new targets for IEPs. Parents should be invited so that they can contribute to this planning process and can be reassured that everyone is aware of their child's needs.

Easing the transition process

Chapter 11: Primary-secondary transition will be very helpful for all children and especially for those with special educational needs who are transferring to other schools. The transition referred to in this section is that of children who are about to start school for the first time, usually in the Reception class.

In some areas, such as the London Borough of Bromley, the LEA appoints key workers to liaise between pre-school settings and schools to facilitate a smoother and better informed transition for special needs children starting school.

In most areas, however, it is still the responsibility of the SEN coordinator of the receiving school to ensure that all the necessary steps are taken to ease the transition for children with special educational needs. This will include such formalities as the handing on of records, IEPs and reports and the identification of resource needs. As already suggested, a variety of meetings and visits will need to be arranged and preparations made before the arrival of any child who is identified as having special needs.

The 1994 SEN Code of Practice, supported further by the 2001 Code of Practice, requires that, if a child with any identified or potential special need is due to start in a nursery or Reception class, then you should ensure that the child's class teacher is able to

- use information from the pre-school setting to provide starting points for the curricular development of the child

- identify and focus attention on the child's skills and strengths to help plan a programme of support

- take appropriate action at the earliest possible opportunity to minimise stress and maximise progress

- use ongoing observation and assessment within the classroom to inform future planning

- involve parents in developing and implementing learning programmes at home and at school.

If a child may have mobility problems, it is essential to undertake a risk assessment of the learning environment and any areas of the school they may visit, so as to ensure optimum preparation and provision. You may need to make minor modifications, such as a hand-rail in the toilet area or by a step. Find out what the child uses at home and what their parents think they may need. If a wheelchair is to be used, then a similar risk assessment will help to ensure appropriate access and support.

The child may need to have a designated learning support assistant. If so, appoint a suitable assistant well before their arrival, who will be fully prepared to give them all the help they need.

It may be advisable to prepare other children in the school for the arrival of a child with special needs, from both a safety and a PSHE point of view.

Finally

Whatever childrens' educational needs, the 2001 Code of Practice and the National Standards provide a sound framework for their inclusion at all stages and it is clear that the earlier any SEN identification and intervention takes place, the smoother the transition into school and between schools will be. Optimum pre-school provision and liaison will enable optimum benefit for the SEN child in their primary school years.

Reference

Karoly L A et al (1998) *Investing in our Children: What we know and what we don't know about the benefit of early childhood interventions*. Santa Monica: RAND.

DfES/Coram Family Foundation (2002) *Intervening Early*. London: DfES.

DfES (2001) *Special Educational Needs Code of Practice*. Ref. 581/2001. London: DfES.

DfEE (2001) *Guidance to the National Standards*. Ref: 0488/2001. London: DfEE.

Thanks to Christine Khan and Annabel Dixon for their contributions to this chapter.

CHAPTER 11

Primary-secondary transition

The transfer from primary to secondary school is a big step for all children. It can be especially traumatic for vulnerable children and those with special needs. The cosy atmosphere of the smaller primary is replaced by the larger, seemingly impersonal, secondary school. Children imagine an impossible workload given by teachers they don't know and who don't yet know them. They worry that they will get lost and won't know anyone and that they won't be able to ask for help. This chapter aims to help ease the transition between schools and to foster good primary-secondary liaison.

Approaching transfer

'All concerned with the [SEN] child should give careful thought to transfer between phases. Advance planning is essential.' (DfES, 2001 – 5:69)

'It is important for placements to be finalised as early as possible in order for any advanced arrangements to be made and to ensure that parents and children feel confident and secure about the arrangements in question.' (DfES, 2001 – 5:72)

The 2001 SEN Code of Practice sets out some practical guidelines and requirements for both schools to follow in preparation for the primary-secondary transition.

The transfer should initially be considered at the Year 5 review meeting, so that there is sufficient time for parents, their child and any professionals involved to consider together what options might be available and thereby to make informed decisions. It should be possible at this review for recommendations to be made and concerns to be shared about the type of provision required. There will be time for parents and child to visit schools and to consider all the options prior to Year 6. If options are not yet clear, or if the child's situation is changing, it may be necessary to hold an interim review in order to reconsider the position and make alternative recommendations before the final decision is made.

If a child has a statement of special educational need, it will be necessary to hold the annual review as early as possible in the Autumn term of Year 6, to give sufficient time for arrangements to be finalised. The Code of Practice states that the child's statement must be amended by 15 February of the year of transfer, in the light of the recommendations made during the Year 6 annual review, the parents' preferences and the response to consultation between the schools and the LEA. The Code goes on to say that all arrangements regarding the child's placement should be completed by the beginning of March.

Wherever possible, the Code recommends that the SEN coordinator of the receiving school should be invited to attend the final (ie. Year 6) review meeting of any child with a statement who is due to transfer at the end of that year.

'It will then be possible for the receiving school to plan a differentiated curriculum response and an appropriate IEP to start at the beginning of the new school year. It will also enable the pupil and the parents to be reassured that an effective and supportive transfer will occur.' (DfES, 2001 – 5:73)

When any child moves from one school to another, it is a requirement that the child's records are transferred within 15 days of the child ceasing to be registered at that school. However, since primary-secondary transfer arrangements are usually known well in advance, it is good practice for these records to be passed on in good time. In the case of the child with special educational needs, it is particularly advantageous to provide as much information as possible to the receiving school well in advance of the actual transfer, to allow appropriate planning to take place. This advance information should include

- any detailed background information collated by the primary school SEN coordinator
- copies of IEPs and targets set and met
- observation and assessment materials
- reports (both in-school and from external agencies)
- copies of statements and any other supporting documents.

All this is the background preparation which needs to take place in the child's final year at primary school. However, there will also need to be an increasingly pro-active programme of preparation for the child, in order to encourage a positive attitude to this major change in their life.

Encouraging a positive attitude

A well-coordinated programme for transition will benefit all children, especially those with special educational needs. If a child is encouraged to feel secure in the transfer and confident enough to face the new challenges, they will continue to learn effectively. This will go some way towards solving the problem of a dip in standards between Key Stages 2 and 3.

Children from primary school are often worried by the sheer size of the new school. The change from one teacher to several takes away the security

required by many special needs children. This is compounded by the confusion of a new timetable and subjects they know nothing about.

Ensuring that every child visits their new school early in Year 6 is a good place to start. Many primary and secondary schools arrange visits so that the children can get the feel of life in the secondary school.

Open evenings

An open evening, where the secondary school puts on an exhibition of all the subjects the children will experience, does much to encourage a positive view of the new school. The children may begin to look forward to the new subjects following the open evening. However, if a few children miss the experience they may feel at a disadvantage, so it is essential that parents are made aware of the importance of their children attending these evenings. In some cases, parents and children may visit several schools, in order to investigate what each school

---

Additional preparation activities for SEN children

For children with special educational needs, it will be helpful to plan some additional activities with the secondary school SEN coordinator and staff, to enable the children to feel more familiar and more at ease with the arrangements.

Orientation sessions – a teaching assistant accompanies each child or group of children, perhaps at the same time as groups from other primary schools. Tasks and challenges are set to familiarise them with the layout of the buildings and where key points can be found. Children can be challenged (and supported as appropriate) to find particular rooms (such as the special needs room, the first aid room or the school's reception area), or to find the shortest route between places (such as between the dining hall and the nearest toilets).

Colour-coding plans of the school – this enables children to see at a glance where subjects are taught (eg. yellow for English, blue for maths) and how to find other key areas (eg. striped for the library).

Early timetables – if possible, special needs children should be provided with their timetables early and go through them in advance with their teaching assistants, to help them become familiar with the pattern of the school day (such as lesson times) and where the rooms are which will be most often needed.

Lunchtimes – as lunchtime is often one of the most baffling times for special needs children, the primary school teaching assistants accompany them to the

secondary school for lunch one day a week for the last month or so, preferably at the same time as groups of special needs children from other primary schools so that they can get to know each other better.

Videos – make a video of various parts of the secondary school campus, also showing special needs children in action in classrooms and around the school.

Pen-pals – Year 7 children with special educational needs write letters and draw cartoons or pictures for their Year 6 counterparts, telling them about their first impressions of moving to the secondary school and giving them advice for making the transition. The older children then act as 'buddies' to their younger pen-pals in their first few weeks at the new school.

ICT joint projects – SEN children in Year 7 at the secondary school undertake an ICT project to communicate and work with Year 6 children in the primary school. This might involve a curriculum subject, or pen-pal communication, or hobbies and other interests.

SEN coordinator visits – the secondary school SEN coordinator visits the primary school to have one or more sessions talking to the special needs children in Year 6, to describe how things will be for them in the new school and to answer any questions. The primary school SEN children have the opportunity to get to know a friendly face, which gives them greater confidence on transfer.

---

would be able to offer them and to be able to make an informed choice between them.

Induction days

Induction days, where children attend the secondary school for one or two days in the term prior to entry, are a great success. It is useful if there is an extra induction day with the special needs staff to ensure that children with special needs are happy with the new school and feel part of the new system. If this is possible, the children can spend the day with the new teachers and older children within the department. Investigate opportunities for parents to meet the staff after the induction day to discuss any problems.

Visits for drama, music or sport

To get away from the more academic emphasis of induction days, special visits could be made to take part in sports, art, music and drama workshops. These will give special needs children the chance to shine in other areas of work, increasing self-confidence and also giving the secondary school staff the opportunity to get to know the children's interests and abilities. Liaise with the secondary schools to see what is available.

Teacher visits

As well as primary pupils visiting the secondary school, it can be very helpful for all children if arrangements can be made for one or more of the secondary school teachers to come and teach lessons to Year 6 in their own primary school classrooms. This has a two-way benefit, allowing the children to get to know an adult who will be a familiar face in the new school, as well as giving the teacher a chance to assess the levels at which the children are learning.

Preparing for difficult situations

Going into a new social situation can throw up a number of worries about what to do if faced with difficulties. Children with poor self-confidence will not always be able to draw on previously learned strategies to deal with problems such as bullying, drugs or smoking or knowing what to do if they miss the bus or train. This can be an overwhelming worry for children who are used to being taken to school in a car or walking a short distance.

A possible answer to this situation is to involve secondary school children and staff during the last term of primary school. A personal and social education programme will already be in place in the

primary school. This will undoubtedly have looked at what to do when faced with bullying or what to say if you are offered a cigarette. The children then often expect to face these situations every day! In reality, of course, this doesn't happen and secondary school children could reassure the younger children that they will not come across such situations all the time. They will also be able to talk to the children about strategies they have used if, for example, a bullying problem should arise.

Children often believe friends and other children more readily than teachers, so it can be useful to involve the older children as much as possible.

A good personal and social education programme will be essential in the weeks leading up to transfer, with a special emphasis on activities which build self-esteem and a concentration on the positive aspects of the child's ability.

Involving parents

Parents of children with special needs should have additional discussions with the SEN coordinator, as well as members of senior staff in the secondary school. This could happen on an informal basis, after the extra induction day for children with special needs described earlier, or appointments could be made nearer the time to meet and pave the way. Concerns about transfer usually centre on the size of the school and whether the child will be able to cope with the work given, although there may be other specific concerns.

It is nearly always of great benefit if a child with special needs knows who to ask for help in given situations. They can also benefit greatly from one identified person being allocated to them as a mentor or support. Finding ways in advance of arranging this and even meeting the people concerned can make for a more confident transition.

Additional liaison and the opportunity to ask questions of special needs staff will go some way to allaying parents' fears for their children at secondary school level. Consider inviting parents to an open discussion and question-and-answer session at school, in which you can share the ways in which they can help, for example by practising the new journey a couple of times at the correct time of day during the summer holidays. There is much that parents can do if they are aware of what the school is working on and are helped to understand their child's areas of concern.

These concerns tend to fall into three areas, which are

1 emotional demands, such as leaving old friends and needing to make new ones or moving from being the oldest in the school to the youngest.

2 study skills, such as taking notes, getting homework in on time.

3 personal organisation, such as thinking ahead about what is needed for the day, finding their way around and not losing bus or train tickets.

> ### Transition programme summary
>
> A good transition programme will include the following.
>
> ☐ Opportunities for Year 6 children to visit the secondary school throughout the year for different types of activity.
>
> ☐ A planned programme of meetings between primary and secondary staff to discuss the liaison which will take place and the individual needs of the children transferring. The SEN coordinator should be a part of these meetings.
>
> ☐ Shared project work to be started in the primary school and followed up in the secondary school
>
> ☐ A well-structured personal and social education programme, giving children the opportunity and confidence to ask questions. Involvement from secondary school children can also be a great help.
>
> ☐ A structured approach to involving parents.
>
> ☐ Additional support for parents of children with special needs. This may involve extra meetings with staff from both schools to reassure them that their children's needs will be met.

Finally

Many of the suggestions given here need time for constructive liaison and planning. This has to be accorded high priority by senior staff in the primary and secondary schools. It is important that the SEN coordinator is a part of these discussions and that they take place early in the transition process.

A well-coordinated approach to the three areas of emotional demands, study skills and personal organisation throughout Year 6, working in partnership with parents, with input that addresses children's specific special educational needs, can help give children a secure start. This start can provide the foundation they need for a successful transition to the next stage of their learning.

The most positive start in a new school can be achieved if children are helped to see this step as an exciting challenge, rather than as a huge mountain to climb. With a carefully planned programme of transition, we can encourage all our children, and especially those with special educational needs, to approach their new school on the first day of term with as much confidence as possible. This confidence will be their main stepping stone to success and happiness through their secondary school years.

Reference

DfES (2001) *Special Educational Needs Code of Practice.* Ref. 581/2001. London: DfES.

Thanks to Gillian Rees for her contribution to this chapter.

CHAPTER 12
Inclusion

Inclusion is now a focus for development in all schools. The recommendations of the 1978 Warnock Report and the statutory requirements of the 1981 Education Act set the trend in promoting the rights of children with disabilities and learning difficulties to have better access to mainstream provision. This process has continued and broadened to include all sections of the community, through a succession of legislation and guidance, culminating in the new 2001 SEN Code of Practice and the 2002 Disability Discrimination Act Part 4 Code of Practice.

All the research seems to agree that children with special educational needs benefit educationally from inclusive education, making greater progress in many areas, especially English (reading, speaking and listening) and study skills at Key Stage 1 and maths and science at Key Stage 2, when they are in mainstream schools.

LEAs have responded to their responsibilities in a variety of ways. Each LEA's approach will affect their region's planning for inclusion and the demands made on their schools. However, schools themselves have the major role in ensuring equality of provision and access.

Inclusion is now accepted to encompass all types of need and difference, including

- gender (girls and boys)
- minority ethnic groups
- faith groups
- travellers
- asylum seekers and refugees
- children who need support to learn English as an additional language
- children with special educational needs
- gifted and talented children
- young carers
- children from families under stress
- pregnant schoolgirls and teenage mothers
- children who are at risk of disaffection and exclusion.

While many of these categories of need and difference may overlap, this chapter will concentrate mainly on the needs of SEN children and what we need to do to include them fully in our mainstream primary schools.

Integration

The Warnock Report raised the concept of integration, recommending that children with special needs should be educated in their local mainstream school wherever possible. The 1981 Education Act required LEAs to integrate children, as long as this met the three conditions that

1 the school could meet the child's needs

2 the child's attendance at the school was not detrimental to the education of other children

3 it was an effective use of the LEA's resources.

It was evident, however, that a child's attendance at a mainstream school didn't necessarily mean that they were a full and active member of the school's community.

Three different forms of integration were defined.

1 **Locational integration** applied to those types of inclusion where a child attended a mainstream school, but was nonetheless socially and educationally isolated.

2 **Social integration** applied to situations where a child was included in a mainstream school and gained from interactions with his or her peers, but followed separate learning programmes.

3 **Educational integration** was the aim – this would be achieved where, due to the approaches adopted by the teachers and the wider school community, policy and circumstances, a child was able to access the curriculum and make progress with his or her peers.

From integration to inclusion

In the mid-1990s, the focus began to shift from integration to inclusion. Successive government publications had moved towards fuller inclusion. International discussions were also taking place regarding the rights of all children, leading to the 'Salamanca Statement', drawn up by the UNESCO World Conference held in Spain in 1994. This called upon all governments to

> '...adopt as a matter of law or policy the principle of inclusive education, enrolling all children in regular schools, unless there are compelling reasons for doing otherwise.'

How do integration and inclusion differ?

The distinction between integration and inclusion is not immediately apparent. In 1997 Gordon Porter (Director of School Studies in New Brunswick, Canada) provided a very useful model to clarify this issue.

Integration	Inclusion
Focus on the child	Focus on the classroom
Assessment of the child by a specialist	Examining teaching and learning factors
Diagnostic/prescriptive outcomes	Collaborative problem-solving
Programme for the child	Strategies for the teachers
Placement suitable to enable the programme to be delivered	Adaptive and supportive mainstream classroom

In 1997, the government published *Excellence For All Children: Meeting Special Educational Needs*. This document set out the strategies required to improve standards of provision for all children with special educational needs. It enshrined a clear commitment to promoting greater inclusion, highlighting the significant educational, social and moral benefits of inclusion.

In 1998, the government published *Meeting Special Educational Needs: A Programme for Action* undertaking to review statutory provision. In response to this document, the Disability Rights Task Force published a report entitled *From Exclusion to Inclusion* in 1999, recommending

> 'a strengthened right for parents of children with statements of special educational needs to a place at a mainstream school.' (Disability Rights Task Force, 1999)

The Special Needs and Disability Act of 2001 delivers this strengthened right, transforming the statutory framework for inclusion (of 1996) into a positive endorsement of inclusion. The Act seeks to enable more children who have special educational needs to be included successfully within mainstream education. The implications are that wherever parents want a mainstream education for their child, everything possible should be done to provide it and where parents want a special school placement, their wishes should be listened to and taken into account.

The Index for Inclusion

Early in 2000, a copy of the *Index for Inclusion* was sent to every school in England and Wales. This document, published by the Centre for Studies on Inclusive Education (CSIE), built on the work of researchers in Australia and North America, who devised indices for assessing the quality of inclusion for children with a variety of impairments.

The *Index* is a set of materials to support schools in a process of 'inclusive school development'. It focuses on building supportive communities and encouraging high achievement for all children and staff.

It is aimed at improving educational attainment through inclusive practice, drawing upon the increasing body of research that indicates that the most effective schools are those that are able to respond to the diversity of their school population. This runs contrary to the perception that the inclusion agenda is at odds with the drive to raise educational standards.

The *Index* makes clear that 'inclusion' is **not** another term for 'special educational needs'. The authors state that inclusive education involves a different approach to identifying and attempting to resolve the difficulties that arise in schools. Further,

> 'The concept of special educational needs is not used in this document since we argue that the approach with which it is associated has limitations as a way of resolving educational difficulties and can be a barrier to the development of inclusive practices in schools. It confers a label that can lead to lowered expectations. In focusing on the difficulties experienced by categorised students it may deflect attention from those experienced by others.' (Booth *et al.*, 2000)

In the *Index*, the term 'special educational needs' is replaced by the term 'barriers to learning and participation'.

SEN coordinator or learning support coordinator?

A number of schools now call their SEN coordinator a 'learning support coordinator' and this term may be helpful in connecting the work with children who experience learning difficulties with broader concerns about teaching and learning. This also has significant implications for the areas of responsibility which go with the role and the potential influence that you, as coordinator, can have upon all aspects of school life.

The Index explores inclusion within the interconnected dimensions of

- **Cultures** – whether the school is creating a secure and stimulating learning environment in which everyone is valued
- **Policies** – how inclusion permeates aspects of the development and implementation of all school policies
- **Practices** – making the school practices reflect the inclusive culture and policies.

One of the most powerful aspects of the *Index* is that the approach is firmly rooted in school development. Integral to the process are five phases.

- **Preparation** – establishing a coordinating group. Members of this group will familiarise themselves with the concepts, materials and methods for gathering knowledge from the school community and will communicate their plans to the rest of the staff.
- **Finding out about the school** – completing an audit of the culture, policies and practices. The coordinating group will make a detailed exploration of the school and will identify priorities for development, which they will then share with the staff.
- **Producing an inclusive development plan** – adapting the current development plan. The group will consider the current school development plan, alongside the priorities identified following their whole-school audit, and will amend the school development plan accordingly to ensure that it reflects the priorities for inclusion, and will share this with the staff.
- **Implementing developments** – an ongoing process, as the school meets its various challenges and changes its culture, policies and practices accordingly.

- **Reviewing the process** – there will need to be a scheduled programme of meetings to review the school's progress in implementing developments.

Using the Index

Through a branching-tree structure, the *Index* suggests a number of practical ways to establish how inclusive a school is and to determine the perspectives of all the relevant interest groups – staff, children, parents, carers and members of the whole community.

The materials are provided in three sections, concerning the building of inclusive cultures, policies and practices. In each section of the *Index*, there are up to 12 indicators, each of which is clarified by a series of questions.

The three examples which follow give one indicator from each section of the *Index* and two or three questions for each. These examples demonstrate in a small way how working with the *Index* materials encourages staff to share and build on what they know about what helps and what hinders the process of inclusive learning in their school community. It is an effective, systematic way of engaging the whole school staff in developmental planning.

Inclusive cultures in school

Indicator Staff collaborate and support each other.
Questions
- Do staff feel comfortable about discussing problems they are experiencing?
- Are all staff invited to meetings?
- Do staff members treat each other with respect, irrespective of their roles?

Inclusive policies

Indicator All new staff are helped to settle into the school.
Questions
- Is there a planned programme of integration for new staff members?
- Do new members know who to turn to if they have a problem?
- Are opportunities provided for new members to raise concerns?

Inclusive practices

Indicator Children are actively involved in their own learning.
Questions
- Do the classroom environment, displays and other resources help develop independent learning?
- Do children have choices within their learning activities?

The *Index* file also includes a number of questionnaires intended to be used by different audiences. In the questionnaire designed for use in primary schools, the children are asked about a range of topics, including

- classroom groupings
- whether friends help them with their work
- classroom rules
- bullying
- homework
- how the teachers follow up after a child has been absent.

Clearly, undertaking the *Index for Inclusion* process demands a high level of commitment from a school and, in particular, from the senior managers. The fact that it is firmly rooted in school development planning and, therefore, part of the school improvement agenda is a strong incentive. The use of the *Index* is undoubtedly a powerful tool for you to influence policies and practice in a school.

Social Inclusion: Pupil Support

In 1999, the Government published two circulars (10/99 and 11/99) which provided guidance regarding the social inclusion agenda and pupil support. This document outlined examples of good practice, recommended provision, potential funding and research findings about Social Inclusion: Pupil Support (SIPS).

The guidance document (10/99) sets out some principles for good practice which have been shown to be effective in schools. These include

- setting good habits early – establishing punctual attendance and good behaviour from the start of school, enlisting the support of parents
- early intervention – where needed, to make the school's expectations clear
- rewarding achievements – positive recognition of individual child, class or year group achievements, including those for punctual attendance and good behaviour
- supporting behaviour management – through such approaches as circletime, 'assertive discipline' and 'circle of friends'
- working with parents – encouraging them to support prompt attendance and good behaviour, through home-school agreements, parents' meetings and newsletters

- involving children – children themselves helping to reinforce school behaviour policies by active involvement in anti-bullying initiatives and by contributing ideas through school councils
- commitment to equal opportunities – sharing the school's equal opportunities policy with both parents and children and its impact being monitored
- identifying underlying causes – there may be reasons for poor behaviour which can be tackled in school, such as difficulty in understanding lessons or instructions
- study support – such as homework clubs or thinking skills workshops
- multi-agency approaches – to underpin the work of schools.

Circular 10/99 also provides a checklist for groups at particular risk, ie.

- children with special educational needs
- children in the care of local authorities
- minority ethnic children
- travellers
- young carers
- children from families under stress.

Looked-after children

Children in the care of local authorities, often known as looked-after children, span the full ability range, but the guidance tells us that up to 75 per cent of them have left school by 16 with no qualifications at all. 25 per cent of looked-after children do not even attend school after 14.

The government set attainment targets for these children in a push to encourage school attendance and raise standards in this group. *Education Protects – Guidance on the Education of Children and Young People in Care* offers more detailed guidance. One of its recommendations is that a designated teacher is needed to take responsibility for the interests of looked-after children in each school. This role will often be taken on by the SEN coordinator. Each looked-after child should have a personal education plan (PEP) drawn up

'...which ensures access to services and support; contributes stability, minimises disruption and broken schooling; signals particular and special needs; establishes clear goals and acts as a record of progress and achievement.' (DfEE, 2000 – 5:17)

Other at-risk children

Circular 10/99 also recommends that a member of staff, often the SEN coordinator, should be designated to monitor the needs of young carers and children from families under stress and to coordinate support for them as appropriate.

Towards inclusive schooling

In 2001 the DfES produced *Inclusive Schooling*, a guidance document which has statutory status. This document sets out the aims and requirements of the framework for inclusion. It makes clear at the outset what all relevant school and LEA personnel should keep in mind.

> **Key principles of an inclusive education service**
>
> • Inclusion is a process by which schools, LEAs and others develop their cultures, policies and practices to include pupils.
> • With the right training, strategies and support nearly all children with special educational needs can be successfully included in mainstream education.
> • An inclusive education service offers excellence and choice and incorporates the views of parents and children.
> • The interests of all children must be safeguarded.
> • Schools, LEAs and others should actively seek to remove barriers to learning and participation.
> • All children should have access to an appropriate education that affords them the opportunity to achieve their personal potential.
> • Mainstream education will not always be right for every child all of the time. Equally, just because mainstream education may not be right at a particular stage it does not prevent the children from being included successfully at a later stage.

Inclusive Schooling promotes the widest view of what is meant by inclusion and how to achieve it successfully in schools.

> 'Schools and local education authorities that are successful at including pupils with special educational needs meet those needs in a positive and proactive way. They also approach inclusion as part of their overall improvement strategy. Inclusion is far more than just about the location of a child's school placement.

Inclusion is about engendering a sense of community and belonging and encouraging mainstream and special schools and others to come together to support each other and pupils with special educational needs. Inclusive schools and local education authorities have

> • an inclusive ethos
> • a broad and balanced curriculum for all pupils
> • systems for early identification of barriers to learning and participation; and
> • high expectations and suitable targets for all children.' (DfES, 2001)

The document makes good use of examples of these four characteristics in action in schools. It also advocates use of the *Index for Inclusion* and the guidance produced jointly by the DfEE and QCA often known as the 'P scales'.

Safeguarding the needs of SEN children

There are several fundamental safeguards in place which must be respected. These are set out in the 1996 Education Act, as follows.

• Parents must ensure their children receive full-time education suitable to their age, ability and aptitude and any special educational needs they may have. This means that parents need to consider what type of provision is most appropriate for meeting their child's needs. Parent partnership services provide information to parents on the options and empower them to make informed decisions (section 7).

• LEAs must have regard to the general principle that children must be educated in accordance with the wishes of their parents, so far as that is compatible with the provision of efficient instruction and training and the avoidance of unreasonable public expenditure (section 9).

• LEAs must ensure that sufficient schools are available for their area and in doing so must have regard to the need to secure special educational needs provision. This should take account of parental preferences for particular styles of provision and education settings (section 14).

• LEAs should, where necessary, maintain statements of special educational needs. Statements specify the provision to be made for a child's special educational needs and LEAs then have a statutory duty to arrange for it to be made (section 324).

- Governing bodies of maintained schools must use their best endeavours to secure that any child who has special educational needs receives the special educational provision their learning difficulty calls for. This includes ensuring that teachers are aware of the importance of identifying, and providing for, children with special educational needs (section 13).
- The Secretary of State for Education and Skills can intervene where LEAs or maintained schools are acting unreasonably or failing to fulfil a statutory duty, or where LEAs are failing to perform their functions to an adequate standard (sections 496, 497, 497A).
- The child's individual needs must be taken into account in deciding whether to name a parent's choice of maintained school (mainstream or special) in a statement (schedule 27).

Children with statements

The starting point in deciding where a child with a statement of special educational need should be placed is always that they will receive mainstream education. Section 316 of the statutory framework for inclusion (Education Act 1996) states that a child with a statement must be educated in a mainstream school unless this would be incompatible with the wishes of the child's parents or the provision of efficient education of other children (if there are no reasonable steps which could be taken to prevent the incompatibility in a particular school or across the LEA's mainstream schools).

When a maintained school or a maintained special school is named in a child's statement, the school must admit the child. Where a child has a statement and the parents do not wish the child to be educated in a mainstream school, then the LEA may educate the child in a special school.

Accessing the National Curriculum

The chapter in the National Curriculum entitled 'Inclusion: providing effective learning opportunities for all pupils' reflects statutory guidance, outlining

'how teachers can modify, as necessary, the National Curriculum programmes of study to provide all pupils with relevant and appropriately challenging work at each key stage.' (DfEE, 1999)

It sets out and explains how to address 'three principles that are essential to developing a more inclusive curriculum.'

1 Setting suitable learning challenges
The basis of this principle is that

'Teachers should aim to give every pupil the opportunity to experience success in learning and to achieve as high a standard as possible.'

This means that teachers are permitted to modify the National Curriculum as necessary.

- Teachers should teach the knowledge skills and understanding in ways that suit their pupils' abilities. This may mean choosing knowledge, skills and understanding from earlier or later key stages.
- For children whose attainments fall significantly below the expected levels, a much greater degree of differentiation will be necessary.
- A flexible approach will need to be used where selecting content from an earlier key stage may mean that not all content can be fully covered or where there may be gaps in children's learning, resulting from missed or interrupted schooling.

2 Responding to children's diverse learning needs
Teachers should consider that not only do children have very differing needs, but they will also come to school with different experiences, interests and strengths which will influence the way they learn.

Teachers should consider to what extent they ensure that

- the learning environment is appropriate to all children
- the children are motivated and able to concentrate
- their teaching approaches provide equality of opportunity
- they are using appropriate approaches to assessment
- they set learning targets.

3 Overcoming potential barriers to learning and assessment
For those children whose requirements go beyond the provisions already described, teachers must take account of these requirements and make provision to support them in order to enable them to participate effectively in the curriculum and assessment activities, including making appropriate special arrangements for National Curriculum tests. Curriculum access for some children may be achieved through greater differentiation of tasks or materials, the use of specialist equipment and approaches or through adapted or alternative activities.

Teachers may facilitate access to learning for SEN children by

- providing support for communication, language and literacy
- planning to develop understanding through the use of all available senses and experiences
- planning for children's full participation in physical and practical activities
- helping children to manage their behaviour so as to be able to take part in learning effectively and safely.

The National Curriculum handbook further states that

'Applying these principles should keep to a minimum the need for aspects of the National Curriculum to be disapplied for a pupil.' (DfEE, 1999)

It includes additional advice and examples to accompany each of these three principles. It will be useful to draw class teachers' attention to this chapter and to consider together, as a whole school, how these suggestions can best be resourced, supported and implemented.

QCA guidance

In 2001, the DfES and QCA jointly produced a set of materials entitled *Planning, Teaching and Assessing the Curriculum for Pupils with Learning Difficulties*, which can be found on the QCA National Curriculum website (www.qca.org.uk). Full sets of these materials were distributed to all special schools, but not to mainstream schools. However, these materials will also be supportive to SEN coordinators in mainstream schools to help them implement the inclusion agenda.

This extensive guidance is introduced with some advice on how to facilitate greater access to the National Curriculum and how to modify the programmes of study. Other sections are considered below.

Determining the curriculum for your school
This section encourages school communities to discuss and develop their own approaches to facilitating curriculum access for SEN children, with some helpful points to consider as a whole staff.

Teaching assistants
Recent research studies have shown that the role of teaching assistants is becoming increasingly important in making inclusion work. Their availability and their skills are invaluable in helping children to access the curriculum. The QCA guidance includes some helpful

case studies of primary-aged SEN children's experiences. The case studies highlight the importance of recognising teaching assistants' close knowledge of their pupils and their needs. The teaching assistants themselves see one of their most important roles as helping interaction between children and between children and staff.

Teaching assistants can only work effectively with the class teacher to support children's learning if they have

- a clearly defined role in the classroom
- time to share the planning of lessons and to report afterwards
- adequate resources (including training and information)
- the importance of their role in the staff team recognised.

Strategies teaching assistants adopt to support learning include

- preparation/differentiation of material before it is used by the SEN child or group
- rehearsal of information after discussion
- summarising the learning points
- reinforcing the learning
- scribing or reading for the child or group
- specialist techniques such as mind-mapping
- differentiation by a variety of other means according to the child's needs.

Planning the curriculum
The useful advice in this section includes planning for progression for children with learning difficulties, which might focus on

- skill development
- breadth of curricular content
- a range of contexts for learning
- a variety of support equipment (to enable children to take control of their environment)
- a range of teaching methods (determined by children's individual strengths and learning styles at different stages of development
- negotiated learning (where children are encouraged to take a greater part in the learning process)
- application of skills, knowledge and understanding in new settings
- strategies for independence (where children are helped to move away from adult support)

131

In practice, all these aspects will be linked to facilitate access to the curriculum.

Recognising progress and achievement

This section focuses on identifying children's needs, the progress they make and the learning preferences they demonstrate.

A framework for recognising attainment will be particularly helpful in recognising attainment below Level 1 of the National Curriculum, including

- encounter
- awareness
- attention and response
- engagement
- participation
- involvement
- gaining skills

The guidance also advocates using the 'P scales' to recognise attainment (see also Chapter 3: Assessment).

The QCA guidance also focuses our attention on the development of skills across the curriculum to include children with learning difficulties. It gives suggestions for and examples of

- **Key skills**
  - communication
  - application of number
  - information technology
  - working with others
  - improving own learning and performance
  - problem-solving
- **Thinking skills**
  - perception
  - memory
  - forming ideas
  - language
  - use of symbols
- **Additional priority skills**
  - physical orientation and mobility skills
  - organisation and study skills
  - personal and social skills
  - daily living skills
  - leisure and recreational skills

Learning styles

In *So Each May Learn*, Harvey Silver suggests that

> '...students who are weak in a particular area might be missing out on important content because there are few opportunities for them to learn according to their strengths.' (Silver *et al.*, 2000)

Silver suggests that many SEN children are unsuccessful, not because they lack innate ability to learn, but because their preferred learning style is either ignored or insufficiently used.

Successful inclusion requires teachers first to identify and then build on children's preferred ways of learning and to use these to help children to

- access the curriculum
- organise their learning
- process the information they have accessed.

There are three principle 'gateways' to learning – the entry points through which information enters our brains. These are visual, auditory and kinaesthetic, collectively known as VAK.

Gateways to learning

Visual learners respond best to images such as pictures, diagrams, charts, the written word, computer animations, videos and films. Visual learners may also be more concerned than others about how they themselves look.

Auditory learners take in information more through what they hear, such as listening to somebody talking, the radio, audio tapes and music, as well as listening to videos.

Kinaesthetic learners learn most effectively through touch and movement. They respond well to the use of learning materials, such as cards and games. They need to feel objects, to use space or to move while they are listening and thinking.

The content of a lesson may be the same for all children in the class, but each child, if given the opportunity to do so, will access this content through their own preferred gateway to learning. If a lesson is mainly delivered in an auditory style, for instance, then only auditory learners will gain the optimum benefit from the lesson.

While most children have preferred learning styles, just a few of them have dominant learning styles. These children will access information through only one of the above gateways. The implication for these children is obvious – if they are not given the opportunity to use their dominant gateway, they will access very little information or learning of any kind.

Kinaesthetic learners in particular tend to be penalised by the fact that adults will often see their need to touch and feel everything and their urge to move around as fidgeting and misbehaviour, thus restricting even further their access to learning.

A lot of work has been done recently in the field of learning styles and multiple intelligences, all of which can be useful focuses for whole-staff training. This would certainly awaken teachers and teaching assistants to the benefits of adapting teaching and support styles to help children with learning difficulties. Teachers will often need to be supported to deliver lessons in a balance of learning styles, within a single session whenever this is possible, or, at the very least, across a period of time.

See also Chapter 4: Strategies for learning.

The 2002 Disability Discrimination Act Code of Practice for Schools

In the next chapter, we take an in-depth look at the 2001 SEN Code of Practice. This document and the 2002 Disability Discrimination Act (DDA) Code of Practice for Schools, published by the Disability Rights Commission, provide a joint approach to ensuring equality of provision and access for all SEN and disabled children in mainstream schools.

The SEN Code of Practice emphasises the strengthened right for SEN children to be educated in mainstream schools. It shifts the emphasis to a partnership and multidisciplinary approach, with greater participation for parents and children, and details the inclusive statutory admission requirements for schools.

The DDA Code of Practice sets out the requirements for those providing school education. The duties make it unlawful to discriminate without justification against disabled pupils and prospective pupils, in all aspects of school life.

The two main disability discrimination duties are

1 the duty not to treat children less favourably

2 the duty to make reasonable adjustments for disabled children.

The DDA Code of Practice defines a disabled person as one who

'...has a physical or mental impairment that has a substantial and long-term adverse effect on his or her ability to carry out normal day-to-day activities.' (Disability Rights Commission, 2002)

As well as physically disabled children, many of whom will have statements of special educational needs, this definition includes those who have

• been disabled and are either in remission or who are no longer disabled

• an impairment which is partially or wholly alleviated by medical or other treatment, but still have the underlying impairment

• severe disfigurements, whether or not their disfigurement affects their ability to carry out normal day-to-day activities

• significant behaviour difficulties, if the behaviour difficulty arises from an underlying physical or mental impairment which is medically diagnosed

• sensory impairments, such as those affecting speech, sight or hearing

• learning difficulties.

Inspections

Inclusion is now a central focus for all inspections by Ofsted. To reflect this greater emphasis on inclusion, all Ofsted inspectors have to participate in special training and new guidelines for inspectors have been written. Whether you wish to be well prepared for inspection, or simply to audit and evaluate your school's approach and provision for inclusion, you can download a document entitled *Evaluating Educational Inclusion* from the Ofsted website (www.ofsted.gov.uk).

This document provides extensive guidance to schools on self-evaluation and to inspectors on inspecting inclusion in schools. This guidance relates to all categories of inclusion, but can at the same time be applied specifically to children with special educational needs and/or disabilities.

During an inspection the inspectors focus particularly on various groups of children, such as those with special educational needs. Evidence will be gathered through discussions with children, parents and staff, looking at children's work, their standards and their progress, evaluating data, observing lessons and other relevant activities.

Some schools may be receiving additional funding to support curriculum or other initiatives and, if this is the case in your school, inspectors will evaluate how effectively this provision is being used to raise achievement and promote inclusion.

Inspectors will test inclusivity by posing a range of questions, including the following.

Are all children achieving as much as they can, and deriving the maximum benefit, according to their individual needs, from what the school provides?

• If not, which children or groups of children are not achieving as much as they can? Why not?

Three key questions

1 Do all children get a fair deal at school?

This relates to

- what they get out of school, particularly their achievements
- the opportunity to learn effectively, without interference and disruption
- the respect and individual help they have from their teachers
- their access to all aspects of the curriculum
- the attention the school gives to their well-being
- whether they and their parents are happy with the school.

2 How well does the school recognise and overcome barriers to learning?

This is about

- the school's understanding of how well different groups do in school

- the steps taken to make sure that particular groups are not disadvantaged in school and to promote their participation and success
- its strategies for promoting good relationships and managing behaviour
- what the school does specifically to prevent and address racism, sexism and other forms of discrimination, and what it does about cases of discrimination that do occur.

3 Do the school's values embrace inclusion and does its practice promote it?

The clues are

- how the values of the school are reflected in its curriculum, resources, communications, procedures and conduct
- how people talk about and treat one another in the school
- the leadership provided by senior staff and the consistency of staff behaviour.

- Is the school aware of these differences? If not, why not?
- How does the school explain differences between groups of children in terms of achievement, teaching and learning and access to curricular opportunities? Are these explanations well-founded and convincing?
- Are there any groups of children who find engagement in the work of the school difficult? How do these children relate to each other, and behave in lessons and more generally in and around the school?
- How effectively do staff guide children who are difficult to motivate?
- Do teachers use methods which enable all children to learn effectively?
- How well do teachers work in conjunction with external agencies and support staff?
- What action has the school taken or is it taking to raise the standards of attainment of children or groups of children who appear to be underachieving or at particular risk? If none, why?
- If the school is taking action, is it appropriate and is it effective or likely to be effective? Are there any unintended consequences? How well are these consequences being handled?

- How well does the school work in partnership with the parents and carers of children with disabilities or special educational needs?

Assessing your own school

By using the various questions and key principles throughout this chapter, particularly those outlined above, you will be able to construct a set of questionnaires, to evaluate the effectiveness of inclusion in your school through its culture, its policies and its practices. Alternatively, you can use those given in the *Index for Inclusion*. As well as discussions with staff (teachers, teaching assistants and other support staff), you will need to consult the children themselves and their parents. You will find it beneficial to involve governors too, as they have the responsibility to facilitate and monitor inclusion throughout the school and to report on it to parents.

Inclusion online

The Becta inclusion website (www.inclusion.ngfl.gov.uk) offers the chance join a discussion group, share good practice, read case studies and browse recommended resources. The site will also keep you up to date with legislation and guidance as well as issues and initiatives.

Finally

Inclusion is not new – many schools have been practising it and developing it very successfully for years and we can learn much from their experiences. Inclusion is an ongoing process, embodying an approach that focuses jointly on the needs and experiences of children and on removing barriers to learning. This is at the heart of all our aspirations in educational practice today, in setting appropriate challenges, raising standards and celebrating the achievements of all our children, whatever their circumstances and needs.

References

DES (1978) *The Warnock Report (Cmnd 7212)*. London: HMSO

DES (1981) *Education Act*. London: HMSO

DfES (2001) *Special Educational Needs Code of Practice*. Ref. 581/2001. London

Disability Rights Commission (2002) *Code of Practice for Schools*, London: TSO

Porter, G L (1997) 'Critical elements in inclusive schooling', in S J Pijl, J W Meijer & S Hegarty (eds) *Inclusive Education: A Global Agenda*. London: Routledge

DfEE (1997) *Excellence for All: Meeting Special Educational Needs*, London: DfEE.

DfEE (1998) *Meeting Special Educational Needs: A Programme for Action*, London: DfEE.

Disability Rights Task Force (1999) *From Exclusion to Inclusion* London: Department for Work and Pensions.

DfES (2001) *Special Educational Needs and Disability Act*. London

Booth, T, Ainscow, M, Black-Hawkins, K, Vaughn, M and Shaw, L (2000) *Index for Inclusion*. Bristol: Centre for Studies on Inclusive Education

DfEE (1999) *Social Inclusion: Pupil Support (circular 10/99)*. London: DfEE.

DfEE (1999) *Social Inclusion: the LEA Role in Pupil Support (circular 11/99)*. London

DfEE (2000) *Education Protects – Guidance on the Education of Children and Young People in Public Care (ref. 0269/2000)*. London

DfES (2001) *Inclusive Schooling (ref. 0774/2001)*. London: DfES.

DfEE/QCA (revised 2001) *Supporting the Target Setting Process*. London

DfEE (1996) *Education Act*. London: DfEE.

DfEE (1999) *The National Curriculum, Key Stages 1 and 2*. London

DfES/QCA (2001) *Planning, Teaching and Assessing the Curriculum for Pupils with Learning Difficulties*. London

Silver, H et al. (2000) *So Each May Learn*. Alexandria: ASCD

Ofsted (2002) *Evaluating Educational Inclusion*. London: TSO

UNESCO (1994) *Salamanca Statement and Framework for Action on Special Needs Education* is available from www.unesco.org/education/educprog/sne/index.html.

Thanks to Frances James, Martin Skelton and Julie Jennings for their contributions to this chapter.

CHAPTER 13
The 2001 SEN Code of Practice

This chapter provides an overview and summary of the 2001 SEN Code of Practice and accompanying SEN Toolkit documentation and also identifies the key issues and the way forward.

The Code of Practice begins with a definition of special educational needs.

> 'Children have special educational needs if they have a learning difficulty which calls for special educational provision to be made for them.' (DfES, 2001)

The fundamental principles upon which the Code of Practice is based are that

- 'a child with special educational needs should have his or her needs met

- the special educational needs of children will normally be met in mainstream schools or settings

- the views of the child should be sought and taken into account

- parents have a vital role to play in supporting their child's education

- children with special educational needs should be offered full access to a broad, balanced and relevant education, including an appropriate curriculum for the foundation stage and the National Curriculum.' (DfES, 2001)

The Code then lists critical success factors.

1 The school ensures that, through its culture, practice, management and resourcing, all children's needs are met.

2 LEAs and schools/settings work together to ensure early identification of needs and appropriate interventions.

3 The wishes of the child are taken into account wherever possible.

4 Professionals and parents work together.

5 Parents' views are sought and taken into account.

6 Interventions are regularly reviewed.

7 There is close cooperation through a multi-disciplinary approach.

8 Time limits are observed by LEAs when making assessments.

9 Statements of special educational needs are clear and detailed, with time limits and monitoring arrangements written in, to be reviewed annually.

In order to meet these criteria, everyone involved in SEN education (the LEA, the whole school staff, the governing body, the headteacher, the SEN coordinator, the parents and educational professionals) has specific responsibilities. The child must also be involved. While the LEA has some crucial statutory duties, this chapter will focus particularly on the roles of people concerned within the school itself.

Governors

School governors have a wide range of responsibilities under the Code.

- The governing body of every school should work with the headteacher to decide the school's general SEN policy and approach – this must include the appropriate staffing and funding allocations.

- Governors have a duty to ensure that the requirement to promote high standards in the school relates to all children, including those with SEN.

- Every school must have a 'responsible person', whose role is to ensure dissemination of information about children with SEN statements – this role is generally taken by the headteacher, but it may be the chair of governors or the SEN governor.

- There should be either a named SEN governor or a sub-committee with specific oversight of the school's arrangements for meeting special educational needs.

- Governors must ensure that any performance management objectives set for the headteacher, relating to the performance of or provision for children, include those with special educational needs.

- Governors must ensure that any self-evaluation or review carried out by the school relates also to provision for and inclusion of SEN children.

- The quality of SEN provision in the school will need to be monitored by the SEN governor or sub-committee on an ongoing basis.

- Governors will need to make SEN provision an integral part of the school development planning process.

- Governors must ensure that teachers in the school are given appropriate training and support to identify and provide for SEN children.

- Governors need to ensure that parents are notified of any decision regarding their child's SEN provision.

- Governors have a duty to report to parents on the implementation of the school's policy for SEN children (in the annual report to parents).

- In those schools where governors are the admission authority, they will have to review and, if necessary, update their admissions policy to ensure equality of consideration for prospective SEN pupils.

Headteachers

Many of the headteacher's responsibilities mirror or complement the responsibilities of governing bodies as set out above.

Additionally, headteachers have a duty to

- manage and monitor all day-to-day aspects of the school's SEN provision

- provide appropriate staffing and funding (and where possible physical space) to ensure optimum support for SEN children

- work closely with the SEN coordinator

- keep the governors fully informed.

Teachers and teaching assistants

Teachers and teaching assistants should be involved in the development of the school's SEN policy. All staff who come into contact with SEN children have a duty to be ensure that they are fully aware of the school's procedures for identifying, assessing and making provision for children with special educational needs.

SEN coordinators

The SEN coordinator must

- work closely with the headteacher, senior management team, teaching colleagues and teaching assistants

- coordinate the work of the SEN teaching assistants in supporting the learning of SEN children throughout the school

- be closely involved in the strategic development of SEN policy and provision in the school

- take day-to-day responsibility for operating the school's SEN policy and for coordinating provision for its SEN children, according to the Code of Practice.

Early years

Now that the Foundation Stage has been identified as a separate unit for all children aged three to five in any setting (including mainstream school nurseries and Reception classes), it is expected that children in early years settings will have the benefit of early identification of their needs and that a response will be made to those needs. Information will be collated and passed on from the pre-school setting to the receiving primary school to ensure a smooth transition and continuity of intervention and support. Section 4.15 of the Code lists the roles and responsibilities of the SEN coordinator in any early years setting.

Strategic planning

The Code demands a major shift in emphasis, demonstrating the importance of the SEN coordinator's role and level of responsibility.

Whereas the 1994 Code stated that SEN coordinators should work closely with fellow teachers, the wording in the new Code is that you should work closely with the headteacher, senior management and fellow teachers. Further, you should be closely involved in the strategic development of the SEN policy and provision. This creates many new opportunities for you to

- contribute to the future direction of the school

- bring to the attention of the senior management team the requirements of children with special educational needs, the training needs of the staff, the need for more support staff, money, time and physical space

- raise the profile of the role of SEN coordinator

- further your own professional development.

137

Additional responsibilities

Alongside the original responsibilities of writing individual education plans (IEPs), collating records and supporting teaching staff, you are now expected to

- observe and teach SEN children in their classrooms
- contribute to INSET for the teaching staff
- manage, support and train any teaching assistants who provide learning support for SEN children.

Most teaching assistants do not work beyond the children's school day and any training will need to be carefully managed if it is not to take too much time away from the children.

Time to fulfil the role

For the SEN coordinator in early years settings the Code asks that the school's management (mainly the headteacher and governors) consider the time needed to carry out the role of SEN coordinator and the potential benefits of the SEN coordinator being part the senior management team (section 4.17).

For the SEN coordinator in the primary school, Sections 5.33–5.36 list the functions for which you need time out of your own classroom. These tasks reflect the changes in the role, the demands and expectations from someone who is a member of the school's senior management team and the extra tasks of managing the teaching assistants.

It is noted that the person taking on this role should not also be expected to take on additional curriculum responsibilities, as the workload is equivalent to that taken on by the literacy or numeracy coordinator.

You should also be allowed time to liaise with SEN coordinators from other schools in order to share ideas, support each other and plan strategically, for example to coordinate approaches to planning and share expertise.

Resources

The Code outlines what resources should be available to the SEN coordinator. You should have access to (but not personal ownership of)

- a room for interviewing people
- a telephone
- ICT management systems
- dedicated administrative support.

There are schools where the headteacher or deputy would be lucky to have all of these, but that shouldn't stop a school from aiming high. Neither

governors nor headteachers can suddenly provide funds or buildings, but their provision should be part of the school's long-term strategic planning. It could be included in discussions when developments are about to happen. It should be on the agenda.

Training

You may need to embark on some professional development to fulfil all these additional responsibilities. Managing people, training adults and classroom observation are all skills that deserve specialist training.

Funding

Funding for all of these changes should be met from the school's core budget. Funding for management responsibilities should not be drawn from any funds earmarked for children with special educational needs. Funding decisions rest ultimately with the governors of the school, in discussion with the headteacher. As a potential member of the school's senior management team, you will have a chance to state your needs and influence these decisions.

The graduated response

Under the Code of Practice these are the steps to be taken in monitoring the progress of a child from the outset, when there is a cause for concern, to the stage reached when a child is issued with a statement.

Raising a concern

1 Meeting the needs of all of the children in the school is up to individual teachers and their skills. Each school will have procedures in place to ensure that all children are progressing as they should and respond to any difficulties a child may have.

2 When a teacher finds that a child is not responding as expected or is having increasing difficulties in learning or behaviour, they will seek advice from you about alternative strategies to try in the classroom.

3 The teacher will discuss with you the strategies that have already been tried. Together, you will judge the progress that ought to have been made by the child. Section 5.42 of the Code describes some of the ways in which adequate progress can be defined. You may jointly decide that something over and above that which is normally available will need to be provided for the child. You or the teacher will speak to the child's parents at this

point to find out if they can help in identifying the reasons for a change in learning patterns or behaviour and how they can support the school in helping their child.

4 If the teachers and the parents agree that interventions that are additional to or different from the school's differentiated curriculum and strategies are needed, this triggers School Action. Take careful note of the phrasing of this (section 5.43).

School Action

5 Information now needs to be collected from
  • the class teacher
  • the SEN coordinator
  • any professional working with the child in health or social services, with the parents' agreement
  • the parents.

6 You can
  • carry out any further assessments needed
  • plan future support with the class teacher
  • monitor and review any action taken.

The class teacher can
  • plan and deliver an individualised programme
  • work with the child on a daily basis.

You and/or the teacher can
  • consult with parents about the plan
  • inform the parents about progress.

7 The School Action might include
  • different learning materials
  • special equipment
  • individual or group support
  • staff development or training in alternative strategies
  • adult time to plan interventions and/or monitor progress
  • occasional advice from the LEA support team.

8 An IEP needs to be kept in order to detail three or four short-term targets, strategies, provision, review dates (at least twice per year, preferably termly), success criteria and the outcome of reviews (including the parents' views).

The IEP should only record details that are additional to and different from the differentiated plan for the class.

The IEP will be discussed with the parents and child as it is drawn up and at review meetings.

9 If the child continues to make little or no progress in learning or in behaviour, the school will need to seek help from outside agencies. This becomes School Action Plus.

School Action Plus

10 Along with outside agencies, you will need to review the interventions already implemented. Those involved in this review could include
  • the class teacher
  • an LEA support teacher
  • education, health or social service professionals
  • the literacy and numeracy coordinators

They can consider
  • the strategies tried
  • the targets set
  • any progress made.

11 A new IEP can be written to include new targets, new strategies and any specialist assessments needed from those already involved with the child, or from other specialists such as educational psychologists. The agreement of the parents must be obtained before doing this. Other practical details will be included as in School Action.

You must record what further advice is being sought and what will happen, in terms of interventions, while the advice is being gathered.

It is the responsibility of the class teacher to carry out the interventions set down in the IEP. They should, for the most part, be carried out by the school, in the classroom.

The parents and the child should be involved in these discussions.

If the strategies employed in School Action Plus do not result in an improvement in the child's learning or behaviour, then a statutory assessment will be made.

Statutory assessment

12 There are no changes here since the 1994 Code of Practice. The school must present its documentary evidence to show what strategies and interventions have been carried out. Evidence from assessments made by other professionals should be submitted and any additional assessments arranged. Section 5.64 of the 2001 Code lists the specific information required. Sections 7.38 to 7.45 also give indications as to the type of evidence that will usefully support an application for statutory assessment. This evidence is crucial to the process and is the reason why good record-keeping is important from the outset, when a concern is raised.

13 During this assessment period, continue to support the child using the processes described in School Action Plus.

14 In exceptional circumstances a child may be referred for statutory assessment as soon as a diagnostic or medical assessment has been carried out. This can be done if the school considers that they cannot meet the child's needs, or that the child needs immediate specialist intervention. You should discuss any such child with the headteacher as soon as the concern is raised.

Statement of special educational need

15 If a statutory assessment results in a child having a statement, the governors of the school are legally responsible for ensuring that the funding provided through the statement is used for the named child. In practical terms this responsibility will often fall to you. Talk with your headteacher to find out how resources and services for your children are funded. The funding and resources supplied by the LEA may be distributed to the school in different ways, for example
  • within the delegated budget for all SEN children
  • devolved for named children
  • provided directly from central funds.

16 Once a statement is made and accepted and the child is placed in a school, you must make sure that
  • the child's records are maintained
  • teachers monitor and review the child's progress on a regular basis
  • the school's usual pastoral and curriculum monitoring processes are used
  • IEPs are in place.

Any change in the child's needs should trigger a review meeting at the earliest opportunity.

Transfer

17 If a child has received any level of special needs support, make sure that all the documents concerning the school's interventions with the child are transferred to the receiving school, whether the family are moving to a new area, the child moves to a new phase of education, or the child needs a different school to carry out the actions on a statement of special educational need. You should send
  • IEPs
  • assessment details
  • background information
  • the statement.

Evidence

Evidence is the information that may be required when you seek statutory assessment. It will also be useful for anyone assessing the child. Full details are in Code sections 5.64, 7.40, 7.43 and 7.44. It will be needed by the receiving school on transfer.

Some of these records will be kept by the class teacher in their usual routines and need only be photocopied for these purposes.

All evidence should be factual, dated and signed. It can be handwritten or printed, but should be legible, professional and grammatically correct. It is available for all parties to read, so consider this as you write.

It should include the following.

☐ **Academic achievements** Include baseline assessment, progress through the Early Learning Goals, National Curriculum levels and National Curriculum test results in all areas, but with particular detail for literacy and numeracy. Samples of work used for the tracking of progress are important, as they can demonstrate more than mere data.

☐ **Assessments** Include educational assessments and those from any other professionals.

☐ **Health** Give a medical history where relevant. Include any significant problems with motor control, spatial awareness, language delays, memory and visual or auditory discrimination difficulties.

☐ **Social, emotional or behavioural development** If any of these areas could be contributing to the child's learning difficulties, give evidence. Keep records of problems in the playground as well as in the classroom. Record difficulties with relationships, social interactions and concentration or any inappropriate behaviours.

☐ **Interventions** List those by the school, health or social services, education welfare services or other education services.

☐ **IEPs** Give details of the school's intervention and provision through School Action and School Action Plus, resources and personnel, targets and reviews.

☐ **Views of the parents and the child**.

If a child has a statement, the new school will have to be named in an amended statement before the transfer takes place, particularly at a phase transfer. You will need to arrange for the review of the statement to take place in the preceding school year, or at the very beginning of the last year in your school, to allow time for this process to be completed.

Working with other agencies

There is an expectation that all agencies will work together to provide a seamless holistic service for children. Chapter 10 of the 2001 Code of Practice goes into detail about the nature of this cooperation. Although the basic content hasn't changed greatly since 1994, there is a sense of shared purpose in the way that it is set out and in the words used. The Code refers to a shared perspective, effective collaboration and mutual understanding and agreement, as well as reminding the SEN coordinator of the need for contractual agreements about service and provision. The child is placed at the centre, as all the services are charged with addressing the needs of children and enabling them to improve their situation.

As SEN coordinator, you are responsible for

- auditing the skills available among the staff of the school and identifying those areas where help and expertise will have to be sought from outside agencies in order to make best use of the resources available

- coordinating the provision for each child, including any decisions that need to be made about this

- using specialist advice at appropriate times, including early identification before School Action Plus is in place

- liaising with the relevant services, such as health services, Child and Adolescent Mental Health Services (CAMHS) or social services, about general issues and about named children, with the agreement of their parents.

The LEA should detail services it offers in its policy. You should be familiar with this and make the necessary service agreements.

Specialist advice can be used for

- advice on preventative interventions, management techniques, materials and strategies

- consultancy

- staff training

- support for curriculum development

- direct teaching

- practical support for class teachers

- clarifying problems

- specialised assessments

- home and school visits.

Monitoring implementation of the 2001 Code of Practice

Use these notes as an action checklist to help you monitor progress in your school.

Updating school policy

Annex A of your copy of the 2001 Code of Practice contains Education (Special Educational Needs) (Information) (England) Regulations 1999. On page 3 of this document is a schedule of all of the facts that the governors have to include in the school's policy. There are 17 items listed. Check all 17 items against your current SEN policy.

IEPs

Check the sub-headings on your IEPs to make sure your forms carry all the necessary details. Sections 5.60 and 6.58 of the Code give details. Group education plans (GEPs) (used when a small group of children share common targets, needing the same intervention strategy) may also be set up.

IEPs or GEPs should be part of the whole-school approach to assessment and target-setting. You may find it useful to discuss this with the school's assessment coordinator.

IEPs should focus on up to three or four key individual targets. While providing an appropriate level of challenge, targets must also be both manageable and achievable. The child's strengths and successes should underpin the targets set and the strategies used.

Progress towards achieving IEP targets can be measured in a variety of ways, focusing on the extent to which

- the child closes the attainment gap with their peers

- the attainment gap is prevented from growing wider

- progress is similar to that of the child's peers who are starting from the same attainment baseline, but less than that of the majority

- progress matches or exceeds the child's previous rate of progress

- greater access has been facilitated to the full curriculum
- there has been improvement in self-help, social or personal skills
- improvements in the child's behaviour have been observed.

Section 5 of the SEN Toolkit provide extensive guidance regarding the management of IEPs.

Section 9 of the SEN Toolkit is a guide to preparing for and conducting annual reviews.

Pupil profiles

These contain the information kept by each school for each child. A pupil profile begins with records from any pre-school setting, details the child's abilities at baseline and so on through the child's school career. It provides a broad picture of the child's educational and social development and is passed to the new school on transfer.

For children with special educational needs the document also needs to include

- information from the child's previous school or early years setting about their progress and behaviour
- information from the current school about the child's progress and behaviour
- information from the parents
- information from health or social services where they have been involved
- the child's own perceptions of their difficulty and how they could be addressed
- information on strategies that enable the child to access the curriculum and life in school (sections 5.25 and 5.26.)

All of this information will need to be available if you are requesting statutory assessment. Keep it up to date, clear and accessible.

Partnership with parents

The Code of Practice recognises the 'unique strengths, knowledge and experience' which parents can contribute to 'the shared view of a child's needs and the best ways of supporting them.' They have a critical role to play and

> 'It is therefore essential that all professionals actively seek to work with parents and value the contribution they make. The work of

professionals can be more effective when parents are involved and account is taken of their wishes, feelings and perspectives on their children's development. This is particularly so when a child has special educational needs. All parents of children with special educational needs should be treated as partners.' (DfES, 2001)

Parents of SEN children may need support to

- recognise and fulfil their responsibilities in supporting their children's schools
- play an active and valued part in their children's education
- gain knowledge of their children's entitlement within the SEN framework
- make their views known about how their child is educated
- gain access to appropriate information, advice and support.

Positive attitudes and easily understood information, procedures and support are cornerstones of successful parent partnerships. Chapter 2 of the Code of Practice lists some useful suggestions for making communications between parents and professionals effective (sections 2:7 to 2:9). Schools will also benefit from working closely with the local parent-partnership service.

Pupil participation

Chapter 3 of the Code of Practice begins with this quote from the United Nations Convention on the Rights of the Child.

> 'Children who are capable of forming views, have a right to receive and make known information, to express an opinion, and to have that opinion taken into account in any matters affecting them. The views of the child should be given due weight according to the age, maturity and capability of the child.' (1989, articles 12 and 13)

The SEN Toolkit Section 4 should be read alongside Chapter 3 of the Code to provide useful amplification of the guidance in encouraging pupil participation.

In schools where pupil participation is already a key feature (through such strategies as a school council and individual target-setting), encouraging children to express their views and concerns and to take an active part in the decision-making process comes naturally and easily. A positive whole-school ethos is very supportive of pupil participation.

Children should be involved in all decision-making processes concerning their educational provision. The Code identifies five major areas in which children should be encouraged and enabled to participate.

1 Setting learning targets and contributing to IEPs.

2 Discussions about choice of schools.

3 Contributing to the assessment of their needs.

4 Contributing to their annual reviews.

5 Being involved in transition planning.

While children do need to be listened to and to know that their views are valued, there is a fine balance between giving the child an informed voice and overburdening them with a process they find daunting or bewildering. However, in most situations and for most children it will be possible to enable the child to participate in ways which support their involvement.

The Code suggests that the school should make opportunities for all children, from Reception onwards, to practise decision-making and verbal self-expression. Children with special educational needs should become progressively more involved in setting and evaluating targets within the IEP process. They should be actively encouraged to track their own progress.

Those children who find it too difficult to contribute directly in a meeting with unfamiliar adults, such as at an annual review, could perhaps be encouraged to participate in different ways. Parents, carers, teachers, social workers or other adults who know the child well could talk to him or her and elicit their views, in order to report them on the child's behalf. Simple questionnaires in words, pictures, signs or symbols could be used to support this process. There is some useful guidance on facilitating children's participation in annual reviews in the SEN Toolkit Section 4.

Finally

Together, the 2001 SEN Code of Practice and the SEN Toolkit provide detailed and helpful guidance to everybody involved in the provision of education for children with special educational needs. Both can be accessed on-line at www.dfes.gov.uk.

References

DfES (2001) *Special Educational Needs Code of Practice.* Ref. 581/2001. London

UN (1989) *Convention on the Rights of the Child.* Geneva: UNHCHR.

Thanks to Lynn Cousins for her contribution to this chapter.

also from *pfp*...

The perfect complement to your handbook, the
Special Needs Coordinator's File gives you

- up-to-date and accessible summaries of research studies and successful new initiatives in the SEN field
- articles written to be immediately accessible, instantly useful and easily understandable
- a range of teaching ideas, resources and support strategies for class teachers and teaching assistants
- fully photocopiable contents
- practical strategies and advice on successfully managing SEN in your school
- jargon-free articles on the latest key issues
- reviews of assessment, ICT and published resources
- an issue per term – that's over 140 pages of practical advice per year.

order now

tel 0845 602 4337   **fax** 0845 602 4338   **web** www.pfp-publishing.com